THE GREATNESS OF A PEOPLE

THE JAMAICAN STORY

COURTNEY HUTCHINSON

BambuSparks
Kingston, Jamaica W.I.

First printed in July 2023

Published by
BambuSparks Publishing
4 Rochester Avenue,
Kingston 8
Jamaica W.I.
www.bambusparks.com

Photos are sourced from Wikipedia under the creative commons license or public domain.

Photos of Dunn's River Falls, Doctor's Cave Beach and the Blue and John Crow Mountains by Sanjay Ross

Photo of Louise Bennett Coverley - used with the permission of the Jamaica Gleaner Company (Media) Archives.

Cover Illustration by Shantae Rowe

Cover Design: Olivia Prodesigns

Typeset and Layout by BambuSparks | www.bambusparks.com

For feedback, bulk orders or speaking engagements, contact the author at hutchinsoncstb@gmail.com.

This book is dedicated to my parents,
Ivy and Wrendel Hutchinson,
who nurtured our family through challenging times and amidst recurring obstacles.
It is also a dedication to my three sons:
Courtney, Sean and Khalil,
who have always been the source of my inspiration and motivation.
I love you all.

Foreword

I received a call to set up a business appointment for a person that I had never met, who was new to the province and needed my guidance. That turned out to be the start of a beautiful friendship, which blossomed into more, and now I have the privilege of calling the author, Courtney Hutchinson, my brother. We navigated some of the challenges to which he alluded in his book, relating to settling in new places, issues with acceptance and maneuvering that gray area in which we attempt to retain our cultural identities. All this, while striving for some degree of conformity, while being proud of, and embracing our heritage.

As we traveled this road together, we discovered our commonalities, and that as immigrants, being a business owner did not differ much from being an employee. From the moment that I met him, Courtney embodied passion for his heritage and we shared a common ideal in the need to ensure that our youth are comfortable in their own skin and felt free to engage at any level. Education has always been considered one of his pillars to success, so it isn't surprising that he uses his skills and experiences, via his book, to educate us on the rich heritage of his homeland, Jamaica.

What I like about Courtney's book is that it lays bare a country that acknowledges its past and has used that past to chart a positive course for its future. He uses historical analyses to highlight the journey of a people, from oppression and subservience to a proud nation, which now uses that sordid history as a symbol of cultural significance and pride. He deftly captures the way colonial influences continue to shape the political, social and philosophical environments of the country today, then cleverly juxtaposes this with the resilience of a people that has carved a national culture of unity and pride.

This book depicts a country that has come full circle, a country that is as rich in history, as it is in resources and culture. It also highlights the way the Jamaican people have coalesced around the arts, sports and food, to nurture a culture that embraces as much inwardly, as it does outwardly, I am very enthusiastic about *The Greatness of a People* and also confident that it will be a source of reference for many students, as well as persons like me, who are keen to learn about this beautiful land.

Michelle Shivbarran, MA, BSc. SRES

Vice President of the Hamilton Caribbean Women's Group;
Board Member for the Hamilton Black History Council
Ontario, Canada

Contents

Introduction

Jamaica is paradise and most of us don't realize the treasure we have until we migrate, have to deal with racism and doing the job of three persons, but being paid for one (which is true slavery). In Jamaica, when we say that someone is a manager, it speaks to managerial duties and exemptions from menial work. In North America, that title sometimes comes with cleaning the toilets and a wage barely above minimum wage. People, who return to Jamaica on holidays, rent cars, stay in hotels, and give every family member and close friends physical and monetary gifts, make extreme sacrifices in order to do this.

People think that "foreign" is paradise but it isn't. Jamaica is. This book is a reminder of who we are, and I am hoping that there are enough persons left in our homeland who want to change the corruption and crime, so that the people in the Diaspora can come back home.

I grew up in Jamaica in an era where people respected each other, looked forward to seeing Jonkonnu at Christmas time, and couldn't wait to celebrate Independence. We grew up having values and we wouldn't allow anything or anyone tarnish our reputation. We grew up respecting our elders and each other, and never passing a fellow Jamaican or even a stranger, without saying. "Good morning". Jamaicans are a proud people who have had challenges, but we have held our heads high because we value each other. We value our history, and we have always looked forward to a bright future for our country and our brothers and sisters.

We are all products of our circumstances and most times, not by choice. I was born at Annotto Bay Hospital, but grew up in Kingston, Jamaica's capital city, and spent the majority of my life in St. Andrew until I migrated. My mother was a teacher at the Buff Bay Primary School in Portland, and my father was a police officer at the Buff Bay Police station. My sister, brother and I, grew up in what would be considered then, a "middle class" environment. I went to Calabar High School and Wolmer's Boys' School, my sister to St. Hughes, and my brother to Kingston College. I was a bit of a radical because I soon realized that the world we were accustomed to enjoying, as a family, was different from the one enjoyed by the average Jamaican. So, I explored and socialized with everyone, sometimes to the disgust of my parents.

My philosophy was that the only difference between people and what they achieved was the opportunities they got. The man selling jelly by the street side is no way different from the CEO of an organization, because had he gotten the same opportunity, he may have done better with his life than the CEO. I worked for some of the larger organizations in Jamaica, and it was with deep regret that I left my home to go into an unknown country in North America. I left because Jamaica was being plagued by a level of corruption and violence that would not, and could not be repaired in my lifetime, or my children's lifetimes.

This book, *The Greatness of a People: The Jamaican Story* briefly describes the evolution of Jamaica, tracing its history, including the earliest inhabits (the Tainos), through to colonialism and slavery and eventually its democracy. It includes short biographies of the guardians of our democracy (our Prime Ministers) and short biographies of our cultural, business, sports icons, and business moguls. Other aspects of our greatness, and our cultural identity include our food, religion, music, and places of significance.

The Greatness of a People is a useful guide to get to know Jamaica and further build brand Jamaica. It should evoke a sense of pride in Jamaicans at home and abroad as it showcases the best of Jamaica, the richness of the island, and some of what makes Jamaica a great nation. This book is a call to remember, to celebrate, and to protect the beauty and abundance of our beautiful island in the sun.

The Greatness of a People is meant to be a rekindling fire for those who have fallen out of love with Jamaica. Yes, Jamaica has its challenges, especially where crime, corruption, and violence are concerned, but don't give up on this beautiful island. Let us pause to reflect on where we have been, celebrate what we have achieved, and fight to preserve the best of what remains.

How to Use this Book

Jamaicans in the Diaspora and at home can use this book to educate the next generation of Jamaicans about the nation's history and richness. The younger generation in the Diaspora may not know their history and cultural heritage as it may not be taught in their schools overseas. If we fail to pass on this knowledge, the next generation of Jamaicans in the Diaspora can quickly lose sight of their cultural heritage.

This book may be read or used as part of Jamaica Day celebrations, or during the period we celebrate Emancipation and Independence (*Emancipendence*). It can be a reference material for diasporic activities and may be used for social studies or by tourists who want to get to know more about Jamaica.

Disclaimer: This book is not meant to be a comprehensive historical treatise on Jamaica's development; neither does it cover all aspects of our greatness. It is a snapshot of our history and shows glimpses of our greatness inclusive of, but not limited to, the guardians of our democracy and our cultural icons. It is an easy read to encourage us to build Jamaica, to preserve its beauty, and to stir us to fight against the forces that are seeking to destroy the beauty of Jamaica.

Similar books that speak to our history, capturing some of our heritage and development are: *Pieces of Jamaica* by David Muir and *Jamaica: The Land We Love* by Katerina Budinova.

PART 1: THE EVOLUTION OF A PEOPLE

A Brief Look at Jamaica's History

CHAPTER 1
Out of Many – One People

The Jamaican National Anthem

Eternal Father, Bless our Land,
Guard us with thy mighty hand,
Keep us free from evil powers,
Be our light through countless hours,
To our leaders, Great Defender,
Grant true wisdom from above,
Justice, Truth be ours forever,
Jamaica, land we love.
Jamaica, Jamaica, Jamaica, land we love.

Teach us true respect for all,
Stir response to duty's call,
Strengthen us the weak to cherish,
Give us vision lest we perish,
Knowledge send us Heavenly Father,
Grant true wisdom from above.
Justice, Truth be ours forever,
Jamaica, land we love.
Jamaica, Jamaica, Jamaica, land we love.

Jamaica's National Anthem tells a story of a people who are shaped in a specific mold and socialized to care and respect every human being and their beliefs. This is further reinforced by our motto: **"Out of many, one People,"** where different groups express diverse views, opinions and beliefs which have dictated the way human beings perceive the origins of mankind; and all groups hold steadfast to their own ideologies. These perceptions have shaped the way we live, the way we interact with other beings, the way we see each other and ultimately the satisfaction we derive from our brief sojourn on this earth. Our place of birth and origin, the culture of the people with whom we were socialized, and the education we received in our formative and subsequent years are usually responsible for our outlook on life and how we see others.

It is not unusual for one to be socialized in a particular way and eventually harbour a different perception of life and beliefs. However, generally speaking, we become what we have been taught, in the same way there is a philosophy which ascribes to the fact that "We are what we eat". The history books report that on May 5th, 1494, Christopher Columbus "discovered" Jamaica. This position can be refuted because the definition of discovery posited by Dictionery.com is "to see, get knowledge of, learn of, find, or find out; gain sight or knowledge of (something previously unseen or unknown)". It can be contested that Columbus did not discover Jamaica. He encountered people on his voyages and captured each country's inhabitants, like the Arawaks or Tainos in Jamaica, as they were then called, who were already living here. They had called the island Xaymaca, signifying the "Land of Wood and Water". This, however, is a story for another time.

The Jamaica Information Service (JIS) in chronicling the history of Jamaica reports that the English attacked the island on

May 10th, 1655, and led by Admiral William Penn and General Robert Venables, they overwhelmed the Spaniards who fled to Cuba. The English, with a view of growing crops that could be sold in England, enslaved Africans and brought them to the Caribbean. They were sold and used to farm the plantations, which at that time were predominately sugar cane. The perception bantered around that slaves were brought from Africa to farm the land is indeed incorrect. The reality was that people were taken from their homes and families in Africa and brought to the Caribbean, to be used as slaves.

The slave trade boomed, much to the growing dissatisfaction of the victims who eventually rebelled, regrouped and orchestrated the fight for their freedom. Worthy of note were Tacky, Sam Sharpe and the Maroons who all featured prominently in these uprisings. These frequent rebellions and the annoyance they wreaked on the captors of an enslaved people, ultimately contributed significantly to the abolition of slavery.

An Anti-Slavery committee was formed which included groups such as the Quakers, who were eventually joined by supporters such as William Wilberforce, James Ramsey, Thomas Clarkson and Granville Sharpe. The bill for the abolition of slavery was passed on January 1st, 1808. The complete Emancipation and apprenticeship process came into effect in the year 1834 and in 1838 full freedom was granted. In spite of this, the transition to acceptance and acknowledgement was a lengthy battle which brought to the fore champions for the cause of freedom such as, George William Gordon and Paul Bogle.

In later years, Sir Alexander Bustamante and Norman Manley championed the cause towards self-government and orchestrated the first general elections under Universal Adult Suffrage in December of 1944. The Federation of The West Indies was formed in 1958, and on August 6ᵗʰ, 1962, Jamaica was granted its independence and The Jamaican Constitution was created, thereby guaranteeing the rights, freedom and privileges of every Jamaican.

In the same way young children and teenagers are impressionable and are easily influenced by the adults they aspire to emulate, so too developing and underdeveloped countries are influenced by "developed countries". These "developed countries' still continue to affect our island home and exercise their influence in both positive and negative ways. Notwithstanding, our little island of approximately 2.7 million people has carved its name in the archives of the history books of the world. Jamaicans have proven themselves as worthy adversaries in any discipline or walk of life that they pursue.

Jamaica's Transition from Slavery

Jamaica's transition from slavery and the residue from the effects of slavery, still in some way continue to affect us. It has been a complex and ongoing process that has shaped the island's social, economic, and cultural landscape. These are some of the key milestones that are worthy of note that came out of the country's post-slavery history:

- The Abolition of Slavery
- The Apprenticeship period
- The Morant Bay Rebellion
- The Rise of Nationalism
- Independence
- Economic challenges
- Cultural Contributions

The Abolition of Slavery: Jamaica, like many other British colonies, was a major centre of the transatlantic slave trade. Slavery was officially abolished in the British Empire in 1833, but it was not until 1838 that the people who were enslaved in Jamaica were emancipated.

The Apprenticeship Period: After emancipation, many newly freed Jamaicans were forced to work as apprentices on the same plantations where they had been enslaved. The apprenticeship system lasted from 1834 to 1838 and was marked by continued protests, strikes, and violence.

The Morant Bay Rebellion: In 1865, a rebellion led by Jamaican labourers in the town of Morant Bay was brutally suppressed by the British authorities. The rebellion led to the execution of over 430 people, many of whom were innocent. This event marked a turning point in Jamaica's history and helped to fuel the movement for greater self-government.

The Rise of Nationalism: *In* the early 20th century, Jamaican leaders such as Norman Manley and Marcus Garvey began to advocate for greater autonomy and self-determination for the island. This movement led to the establishment of the People's National Party (PNP) in 1938, which played a pivotal role in Jamaica's independence.

Independence: Jamaica gained independence from British rule on August 6th, 1962, becoming the first English-speaking country in the Caribbean to achieve this feat. The first Prime Minister of independent Jamaica was Sir Alexander Bustamante, the founder of the Jamaica Labour Party (JLP).

Economic Challenges: In the years after independence, Jamaica faced numerous challenges, and economic challenges were one of those that marked the development of the era. Some of these included unemployment, inflation and high debt. The country has struggled and still struggles to achieve sustained economic growth and the existence of poverty and inequality remain major issues, thereby continuing to mar our development.

Cultural Contributions: In spite of our overwhelming challenges, Jamaica has made significant contributions to global culture, particularly in the areas of music and sports. Jamaican music genres such as reggae, ska, and dancehall, have had a profound impact on popular music around the world, while Jamaican athletes have achieved great success in events like track and field, bobsledding, and soccer.

A review of Jamaica's transition from slavery to the present day has been marked by struggles and triumphs; and the country continues to grapple with issues of poverty, inequality and political instability. However, Jamaica's rich culture and resilient spirit have helped to shape its identity and inspire people around the world. There is an old adage that speaks to who we are and what we have accomplished during our historic journey, and that is "we likkle but we tallawah". This simply means, never understate or undermine us as a people, because we always have the propensity to bounce back.

CHAPTER 2

The Journey – What Shapes the Jamaican People

The Jamaican people have been shaped by a variety of historical, cultural, economic, and social factors from slavery to the present day. We shall now visit some of these elements, and briefly show how they impacted our development and growth.

Slavery and Colonialism

The legacy of slavery and colonialism has had a profound impact on our Jamaican society. The forced labour of enslaved Africans on sugar plantations created a racialized class system that persists even to the present day. The exploitation and abuse of black Jamaicans by white colonial powers have also left a deep imprint on the national consciousness.

The Psycho-Social Effects

The psycho-social effects of slavery and colonialism have had a lasting impact on Jamaica's development to the present day; and residues of these effects are still evident. Some of the ways these effects have influenced our developments are identified below:

Trauma: The experience of slavery and colonialism left a lasting impact on Jamaica's collective psyche. The trauma of slavery has been passed down through generations, resulting in ongoing emotional and psychological distress for many Jamaicans. This trauma has been linked to issues such as poverty, violence, and mental health problems. The residue left behind from the effects of enslavement continues to rupture the underlying emotional scars that exist, which affects ones sense of value, and self-worth. This can be seen in the widespread practice of bleaching (using chemicals to change dark skin colour to a lighter hue).

Identity: The legacy of slavery and colonialism has also influenced Jamaican identity. Many Jamaicans have struggled to reconcile their African and European heritage, leading to a sense of cultural dislocation and confusion. This has contributed to a search for a distinct Jamaican identity, which has been expressed through cultural forms such as music and literature.

Power dynamics: The power dynamics established during slavery and colonialism continue to shape Jamaica's social and economic structures. The legacy of slavery has contributed to a system of social and economic inequality, with a small elite holding much of the country's wealth and power. This is not unusual, because internationally there are several financial institutions that ascribe to the fact that half the world's wealth is owned by the wealthiest 1 per cent of the world's population (Robert Frank-published Tuesday Nov.14th, 2017). This has resulted in ongoing tensions and social unrest throughout the world, and no less in our island home.

Resistance and resilience: Despite the many challenges faced by our people in the aftermath of slavery and colonialism, there has also been a strong spirit of resistance and resilience. This has been expressed through various forms of activism and cultural expression, including Rastafarianism and reggae music. These movements have helped to foster a sense of pride and empowerment among Jamaicans and have contributed to the country's ongoing development.

The psycho-social effects of slavery and colonialism have had a significant impact on our country's development, shaping the country's identity, power dynamics, and social and economic structures. While these effects have been largely negative, Jamaicans have also demonstrated remarkable resilience and resistance in the face of adversity.

Socio-Cultural Effects of Slavery

The socio-cultural effects of slavery and colonialism have also impacted Jamaica's development from slavery to the present day. Listed below are some of the ways in which these effects have influenced the socio-cultural landscape, then, and now:

Cultural Hybridity: The blending of African and European cultural traditions during slavery and colonialism has resulted in a unique Jamaican culture that is characterized by diversity and hybridity. This cultural fusion is reflected in Jamaican music, dance, cuisine, language, and religious practices.

Racism and Colorism: Slavery and colonialism contributed to the development of a social hierarchy based on race and skin color. Lighter-skinned Jamaicans were often afforded greater privileges and opportunities than darker-skinned Jamaicans. This legacy of colorism continues to shape social and economic inequalities in Jamaica today. This also fuels the culture of "bleaching" (using chemicals to lighten one's dark skin colour).

15

Religion: Religion has played a significant role in Jamaican society, with Christianity being the dominant faith. However, there are also various other religious traditions that are practiced in Jamaica, including Rastafarianism and Obeah, which have emerged as expressions of resistance against the dominant culture.

Language: Jamaica has developed its own unique creole language, which is a blend of African, European, and indigenous languages. Jamaican Patois is widely spoken across the island and has become an important marker of Jamaican identity. Louise Bennett (Miss Lou), succeeded in giving our dialect international recognition and popularity, and indelible in our memory is her introducing some of her pieces by stating "Mi Auntie Roachy sey".

Gender Roles: Gender roles in Jamaica have been influenced by slavery and colonialism. Women were often relegated to domestic and agricultural work, while men held positions of power and authority. However, there has been a growing movement for gender equality in Jamaica, with women becoming increasingly involved in politics, education, and other areas of public life.

The socio-cultural effects of slavery and colonialism have shaped Jamaica's development, contributing to the emergence of a unique Jamaican culture, social and economic inequalities, and ongoing struggles for gender and racial equality. Senior managerial positions still reflect this inequality, but there is a paradigm shift afoot, and we will soon see a difference in this manifesting itself.

Geo-Political Influences

The geopolitical effects of slavery and colonization have had a lasting impact on Jamaica's development, shaping the country's political, economic, and social structures. Despite these challenges, Jamaica has demonstrated remarkable resilience and has emerged as an important player in the Caribbean and global arena. Here are some of the ways in which geopolitics has influenced Jamaica's geopolitical landscape:

Colonization: Jamaica was colonized by the British for over 300 years, which resulted in the establishment of a British-style political system and the imposition of British laws and customs. This legacy of colonization has shaped Jamaica's political and legal systems, as well as its economic and social structures. The existence of a Governor General is a living testimony of the residues of colonialism.

Trade: Jamaica was a major centre of the transatlantic slave trade, with enslaved Africans being brought to the island to work on sugar plantations. This trade in human beings had a significant impact on Jamaica's economic development, as sugar became the country's primary export and source of wealth.

Independence: Jamaica gained its independence from Britain in 1962, which marked a significant turning point in the country's geopolitical history. Since independence, Jamaica has pursued a non-aligned foreign policy, maintaining close ties with both the United States and other countries in the Caribbean and Latin America.

Tourism: Tourism has become an important part of Jamaica's economy, with visitors coming from all over the world to enjoy the country's beaches, culture, and music. The growth of tourism has had a significant impact on Jamaica's geopolitical relations, as the country seeks to attract visitors while also protecting its natural resources and cultural heritage. Tourism has indeed played a significant role in the growth of our economy and continues to be a major foreign exchange earner, and an ongoing means of projecting "Brand Jamaica".

Diaspora: Jamaica has a significant Diaspora population, with Jamaicans living all over the world. The Diaspora has played an important role in shaping Jamaica's geopolitical relations, as Jamaicans living abroad maintain close ties with their homeland and contribute to its economic and social development. In fact, remittances from the Diaspora have greatly contributed to our sustenance especially during times of trial. This book seeks to show appreciation for this group of Jamaicans and well-wishers, who are providers of remittances and wishes to continually encourage them to be a part of our growth and development.

National Heroes: There have been many figures throughout Jamaica's history that have fought for greater freedom, equality, and justice. National heroes like Paul Bogle, Nanny of the Maroons, Marcus Garvey, and Bob Marley have inspired generations of Jamaicans to stand up for rights and fight against oppression. All our National Heroes made valid contributions to our present status as a people, but special mention has to be paid to Marcus Garvey who arranged the first American black nationalist movement. On August 1st, 1914, he founded the Universal Negro Improvement and Conservation Association, and African Communities League, commonly called the Universal Negro Improvement Association (UNIA).

Music: Jamaican music has been a powerful force in shaping the national identity and global perception of Jamaica. From ska and reggae, to dub and dancehall, Jamaican music has been a vehicle for expressing the struggles, triumphs, and joys of the Jamaican people. Over the years, our music has continued to be refreshed, and continues to blossom, bloom, and grow into memoirs for generations to come.

Sports: Sports, and in particular track and field, have been a source of national joy and identity for Jamaicans. The success of athletes like Merlene Ottey, Herb McKinley, Donald Quarrie, Usain Bolt, Asafa Powell, Shelly-Ann Fraser-Pryce, and Elaine Thompson-Herah has helped to elevate Jamaica's global profile and inspire young people across the island, and all over the world. The world records and world leading times for the 100m and 200m sprints are held by Usain Bolt; and another Jamaican, Yohan Blake, has the second fastest time in the history of the event (at the time of writing this book). This is who we are, resilient, hard working, and proud of our heritage and legacy.

Migration*:* Almost anywhere in the world you go, you will find a Jamaican, because Jamaicans have migrated to various parts of the world, including the United States, Canada, the United Kingdom, and other Caribbean countries. This Diaspora has helped to spread Jamaican culture and influence globally.

Globalization

Globalization has had a significant impact on our transition from slavery to the present day. The country's economy and culture have been shaped by various global influences over the years, including trade, technology, and tourism. Here are some of the ways globalization has affected Jamaica's development:

- ***Trade:*** Globalization has led to increased trade opportunities for Jamaica, which has benefited the country's economy. The country has been able to export its products, such as coffee and bauxite to markets around the world. However, globalization has also made Jamaica vulnerable to fluctuations in global commodity prices, which can impact the country's economic growth.

19

Another negative impact, which continues to destroy our country, literally, and figuratively, is the introduction of guns. Jamaica does not manufacture guns, but in spite of that, the number of guns in Jamaica fuelling crime, and killing our people, is immeasurable. North American countries tend to repeatedly mention crime in our country, but they never make mention that the weapons, in most instances, emanated from North America, because Jamaica does not have the capacity to manufacture these weapons.

- *Tourism:* Globalization has played a significant role in the growth of Jamaica's tourism industry. The country is a popular destination for tourists from around the world, and the industry has become a major source of revenue for the country. However, there have also been negative impacts on the environment and local communities, including the displacement of residents and the destruction of natural habitats.

- *Technology:* Globalization has brought advances in technology to Jamaica, which has helped to modernize the country's infrastructure and industries. The adoption of new technologies has improved efficiency in various sectors, including transportation and telecommunications. However, there are also concerns about the digital divide and the impact of technology on traditional industries and jobs.

- *Culture:* Globalization has had a significant impact on Jamaica's culture, which has become increasingly influenced by global trends. Jamaican music, including reggae and dancehall, has become popular worldwide, and the country has gained a reputation as a hub of creativity and innovation. However, there are also concerns about the loss of traditional cultural practices and the impact of globalization on local communities. The international influence has somehow taken away some of our original historical and cultural practices and has somehow replaced them with outside cultural norms that do not represent who we really are.

Generally, globalization has had both positive and negative impacts on Jamaica's transition from slavery to the present day. While the country has benefited from increased trade, tourism, and technology, there are also concerns about the impact of these global influences on the country's environment, economy, and culture, and ultimately, the lives of our people and the generations to come.

The Jamaican people have been shaped by a diverse array of cultural, social, and historical factors. Starting with the struggles of slavery and colonialism to the triumphs of independence and cultural achievement, the Jamaican people continue to shape their own destiny and inspire others around the world.

CHAPTER 3
The Fight for Independence

The transition of power from the Spaniards to the British in May of 1655 brought with it a new paradigm in the shaping of the island's future. The main focus of the British was the growing of crops such as cocoa, indigo, tobacco and sugar cane which was used in the manufacture of sugar. In order to achieve this, they needed labourers in furtherance of their goals. The Africans were found to be hardy workers for the climate, and the slave trade boomed as Africans were shipped from their homeland and brought to the West Indies to be used as slaves. The slave trade was a lucrative and profitable trade for the colonies.

In spite of the fact that the British fleet had more weapons than the slaves, the poor and inhumane living conditions and treatment that were meted out to the slaves created fuel for rebellion. At the time of the British invasion, which resulted in the Spaniards fleeing to Cuba, the Spaniards freed their slaves who sought refuge in the mountains and later became known as the Maroons. The Maroons became and continued to be a constant thorn in the sides of the British. Runaway slaves sought refuge in the mountains and joined forces with the Maroons and increased their harassment of the British forces.

Rebellions became commonplace and there are some noticeable landmark victories that stood out and marked the path to freedom, including:

- The Easter Rebellion of 1760 led by Tacky.
- The Christmas Rebellion of 1831 led by Sam Sharpe.
- The Maroon Wars of 1739 and 1740.

The persistence of the Maroons resulted in the British giving them lands and rights as free men in the treaty of 1740, on condition that they would stop fighting and hand over runaway slaves to the British. There was disagreement amongst the Maroons as some objected to the handing over of runaway slaves. These frequent rebellions contributed significantly to the abolition of slavery and ultimately the slave trade.

Jamaica gained its independence from Great Britain on August 6th 1962, after years of struggle and efforts by its people, as highlighted before in this chapter. There are some factors that aided in Jamaica's fight for independence which were instrumental in impacting the movement in a very positive way. These included, but were not limited to:

- Nationalism
- Political movements.
- Economic pressures
- International pressure
- Leadership

Nationalism: The rise of nationalism among Jamaicans was a major factor in the push for independence. The Jamaican sense of pride and self-worth in their identity and culture, fuelled the desire for self-rule.

Political Movements: The emergence of the political movements such as the People's National Party (PNP) and the Jamaica Labour Party (JLP) provided a platform for Jamaicans to voice their desire for independence. These parties organized mass protests and other actions to advocate and push for greater autonomy.

Economic Pressures: Jamaicans began to realize that the country's economy was constantly being exploited by foreign powers; and that independence would give them greater control over their own resources. They also saw that other previously colonized countries were experiencing economic success and gaining independence.

International pressure: The global trend towards decolonization and the increasing pressure from international organizations such as the United Nations also helped Jamaica's cause. The UN passed several resolutions calling for the end of colonialism and supporting the right of self-determination for colonized peoples.

Leadership: The country was fortunate to have strong and charismatic leaders who were able to mobilize the population and lead the fight for independence. Norman Manley and Sir Alexander Bustamante were both instrumental in pushing for greater autonomy and eventual independence.

Jamaica has had many prominent leaders and prime ministers since Independence beginning with Norman Washington Manley until the now reigning Prime Minister being The Most Honourable Andrew Michael Holness. Amongst these persons who were saddled with the responsibility of grooming the nation for the good of its people, was an outstanding woman, Portia Simpson-Miller, who became our tenth Prime Minister, and the only female prime minister to date. These "Honourable" individuals have helped to shape the island from where it was to where it is today.

The struggle for Jamaican independence was a complex and multifaceted process that involved many factors and individuals. The efforts of the Jamaican people, coupled with favourable international conditions and effective leadership, ultimately led to the country's successful fight for independence.

The global trend towards decolonization and the increasing pressure from international organizations such as the United Nations also helped Jamaica's cause. The UN passed several resolutions calling for the end of colonialism and supporting the right of self-determination for colonized peoples. The country was fortunate to have strong and charismatic leaders who were able to mobilize the population and lead the fight for independence. In our next chapter, we will highlight some of the guardians of Jamaica's democracy.

CHAPTER 4
The Guardians of Our Democracy

The journey from slavery to independence and subsequently self-sufficiency was a tedious one, lined with obstacles and challenges. Overall, the struggle for Jamaican independence was a complex and multifaceted process that involved many factors and individuals. The efforts of the Jamaican people, coupled with favourable international conditions and effective leadership, ultimately led to the country's successful fight for independence.

The emergence of the political movements such as the People's National Party (PNP) and the Jamaica Labour Party (JLP), provided a platform for Jamaicans to voice their desire for independence. These parties organized mass protests and other actions to advocate and push for greater autonomy. Jamaicans began to realize that the country's economy was constantly being exploited by foreign powers, and that independence would give them greater control over their own resources. They also saw that other formerly colonized countries were experiencing economic success and gaining independence.

This section provides a brief biography of the Prime Ministers of Jamaica based on information in the public domain (Wikipedia) and from the Jamaica Information Service.

Norman Washington Manley, M.M., Q.C., B.C.L., LLD (Hon)

He was a noted politician, statesman and national hero, who played a pivotal role in the country's struggle for independence from British colonial rule. He was born on July 4th, 1893, in Roxborough, Manchester, Jamaica, and died on September 2nd, 1969, in Kingston Jamaica. His father was Thomas Albert Samuel Manley, a businessman, and his mother was Margaret Shearer.

Norman Manley was a founding member of the People's National Party (PNP), which was established in 1938. In 1955, Manley became the premier of Jamaica, and in that role, he led the country to independence from Britain in 1962. He was also instrumental in the establishment of the Caribbean Community (Caricom), a regional organization designed to promote economic and political cooperation among Caribbean countries.

The Trade Union Movement in Jamaica was spearheaded by Norman Manley and his cousin, Sir Alexander Bustamante, who had a profound impact on the shaping of the country, and they were considered the "Founding Fathers "of Jamaica's

Independence. In Manley's last public address, with passion and fervour he stated:

"I say that the mission of my generation was to win self-government for Jamaica, to win political power which is the final power for the masses of my country from which I spring. I am proud to stand here today and say to you who fought that fight with me, say it with gladness and pride, mission accomplished for my generation".

"And what is the mission of this generation? It is reconstructing the social and economic society and life of Jamaica".

Norman Manley was named a National Hero of Jamaica after his death on September 2nd, 1969. He was 76 at the age of his death and the foundation he laid was profound.

Sir William Alexander Bustamante, G.B.E., LLD (Hon)

According to JIS, born William Alexander Clarke on February 24th, 1884, in Hanover, Jamaica, and died on August 6th, 1977. Sir Alexander Bustamante became Jamaica's first Prime Minister when he was officially, appointed on the day of Independence, August 6, 1962. He went on to serve as Prime Minister until February 27th, 1967.

Alexander Bustamante had three sisters and one brother. He

was a tall man who towered over his siblings at a height of 6'5". He championed the cause of the common man and was looked upon as somewhat of a hero, and to some extent, a legend. The irony of it all was the fact that he was later conferred with the title and honour of National Hero. As stated earlier, both Alexander Bustamante and Norman Manley were considered to be the architects and "Founding Fathers" of Jamaica's Independence. Bustamante was a charismatic figure who championed the cause of the working class in Jamaica. He founded the Jamaica Labour Party (JLP) in 1943 and led it to victory in the 1944 general election becoming the first Chief Minister of Jamaica.

After Jamaica's independence in 1962, Bustamante became the country's first Prime Minister, and his primary focus was to develop the country's infrastructure, including building new schools, hospitals, and housing developments. He also established Jamaica's national airline and worked to expand the country's tourism industry. He was knighted by Queen Elizabeth in 1967, the same year that he retired from active politics. He made his departure from this world in 1977.

Bustamante was known for making quotes on situations and circumstances that affected him and the people he represented. One of his most famous quotes and one that shows the passion with which he viewed his beloved country was: "Let us resolve to work together under the law to build a Jamaica which will last and of which we and the generations to follow may be proud."

Donald Burns Sangster, ON, GCVO

Donald Burns Sangster, who served as the second Prime Minister of Jamaica, was born on October 26th, 1911, in Saint Elizabeth Jamaica, and died on April 11th, 1967. Son of W. B. Sangster and Cassandra, Donald served on several boards and attended several international conferences on behalf of the country. An avid supporter of the Jamaica labour Party, and Sir Alexander Bustamante, Sangster served as Deputy Leader between the years 1949-1967. He was a Solicitor and was called to the Bar in 1937.

When the first Prime Minister, Sir Alexander Bustamante retired due to ill health, Donald Sangster succeeded him as Prime Minister. During his brief tenure as Prime Minister, Sangster focussed on economic development, industrialization and modernizing the country's infrastructure. He became ill and was forced to resign in February 1967. He died on April 11th, 1967, at the age of 55.

Sangster is remembered as a statesman who played an important role in the early years of Jamaica's independence and helped to shape the country's economic and politic future. To honour him, Jamaica's second international airport, the Sangster International Airport has been named in his honour.

Hugh Lawson Shearer, ON, OJ.

Hugh Lawson Shearer was a politician and trade union leader who served as the third Prime Minister of Jamaica from 1967 to 1972. Hugh Shearer served his country with distinction. Shearer was born on May 18th, 1923, in Martha Brae, Trelawny, and died on July 15th, 2004.

Shearer started his career as a union organizer in the 1940's and he played a key role in the establishment of the Bustamante Industrial Trade Union (BITU), which became one of the largest and most powerful unions in the country.

He was the chief champion at the time to introduce highways in Jamaica. These were designed to alleviate the rising traffic congestions. He served in various government positions, including Ministry of Labour and Social Security before being appointed to the position of Prime Minister following the resignation of Donald Sangster.

Shearer resigned as Prime Minister in 1972 and was succeeded by Michael Manley. He continued to serve in politics and was appointed as Jamaica's first ambassador to the United

States in 1974. He retired in 1980 but remained an influential figure in the Jamaica society. He died on July 15th, 2004.

Michael Norman Manley, ON, OM, OCC

Michael Norman Manley served two terms as Prime Minister of Jamaica, becoming Jamaica's fourth and sixth Prime Minister. He was born on December 10th, 1924, in the parish of Saint Andrew, and died on March 6th, 1997. The son of Edna Manley, and Norman Manley, he was a member of the Royal Canadian Air Force in World War 11 and subsequently attended London School of Economics. The history books record the periods of his being at the helm of the government as being 1972 -1980, and from 1989 -1992.

He became the leader of the Peoples National party (PNP) in 1969 and was elected as Prime Minister in 1972, succeeding Hugh Shearer. As Prime Minister of Jamaica, Manley implemented a series of social and economic reforms aimed at reducing poverty and promoting social justice. He introduced a minimum wage law, established a National Health Service and launched a programme to provide housing for low-income Jamaicans. He also pursued a foreign policy based on non-alignment and sought to build closer ties with other developing countries. He played a key role in the establishment of the Caribbean Community and Common Market (CARICOM).

Michael was a trade unionist and embraced the philosophy of Democratic Socialism. He was also an avid writer who boasts quite a few publications including:

- *Jamaica-Struggle in the Periphery.*
- *A History of West Indies Cricket.*
- *Up the Down Escalator.*
- *Search for Solutions.*
- *The Politics of Change.*

He died on March 6th, 1997. To this day he has left a legacy as being one of, if not, the most popular Prime Minister in Jamaica's history and he was nicknamed "Joshua", which likened him to a prophet in the Bible. This nickname reflected the esteem in which he was held by the people of the country, as he had tirelessly promoted social justice in order to improve the lives of ordinary Jamaicans.

Edward Phillip George Seaga, ON, P.C., LL.D. (Hon)

Jamaica's fifth Prime Minister, Edward Phillip George Seaga was a statesman. In 1952, he graduated from Harvard University in the United States with a degree in Social Sciences. Edward Seaga was born on May 28th, 1930, in Boston, Massachusetts, United States, and died on May 28th, 2019. Seaga became leader of the Jamaica Labour Party in 1974, and subsequently became Jamaica's fifth Prime Minister in 1980. He served two consecutive terms between the years 1980 to 1989.

He was a member of the Jamaica Labour Party (JLP) and served in the Jamaican Parliament for over 40 years from 1959 to 2005. As Prime Minister, Seaga pursued a conservative economic policy based on free market principles, and his policies helped to stabilize the Jamaican economy after a period of economic turmoil. He introduced a series of economic reforms aimed at attracting foreign investment and creating jobs. He founded the Jamaica Cultural Development Commission and the Jamaica Music Industry Association, and he worked to promote reggae music and other forms of Jamaican culture around the world.

One of his crowning legacies was the transformation of the inner city and particularly his constituency in West Kingston of Tivoli Gardens. He devoted forty years in that constituency and was revered by the citizens in and out of his constituency, and ultimately the whole country. He gained notable recognition also for his contribution to the cultural development of the country.

Seaga has been married twice and is the father of four children. Some of the books that he wrote are:

- *The Grenada Intervention -The Inside Story*
- *Institutional Improvements for Development Planning*
- *Clash of Ideologies*
- *Hard Road to Travel*

Percival Noel James Patterson, ON, OCC, PC, QC

Jamaica's sixth Prime Minister, Percival James Patterson was born on April 10th, 1935, in the parish of Hanover and served the country between the years 1992 to 2006. Patterson was noted as an extremely astute politician, and in this vein, became the only politician in Jamaica to have served three terms in office.

A graduate of The University of The West Indies and London School of Economics in England, P.J., as he was affectionately called, was a diplomat whose words were always measured and well thought of. It is this quality which allowed him to defuse several potentially explosive conflicts at home and abroad. Patterson began his political career in the 1950's and was a key figure in the Peoples National Party (PNP). P.J. became the leader of the PNP in 1992 and was appointed as Prime Minister following the retirement of Michael Manley. He was re-elected in 1997 and 2002, and served as Prime Minister until he retired in 2006.

Patterson is widely respected for his contribution to Jamaica's development, and he is known for his strong commitment to social justice and economic progress. He has received numerous awards and honours, including the Order of the Caribbean Community, and the United Nations Environmental Leadership Award.

P.J was called to the bar in 1963, and still offers consultancy services as a senior partner in the law firm, Rattray, Patterson, Rattray. Patterson got married to Shirley Field-Ridley in 1960 and is the father of two children Richard and Sharon.

Orette Bruce Golding, ON

Bruce Golding served as the ninth Prime Minister of Jamaica from 2007 to 2011. He was born on December 5, 1947, in Clarendon, Jamaica. Golding started his political career in the 1970s as a member of the Jamaica Labour Party (JLP). He served as a Member of Parliament (MP) for the West Kingston constituency from 1972 to 1983 and then again from 1989 to 2011. He has had a very long political career being appointed to the Central Executive at the age of 21, and subsequently became Member of Parliament in 1972.

In 2002, Golding was elected as the leader of the JLP, defeating former Prime Minister Edward Seaga. Golding returned to the leadership position of the JLP in 2007 and led the party to victory in the general elections held that year. He was sworn in as Prime Minister on September 11, 2007. During his tenure, he focused on reducing crime, stimulating economic growth, and improving social services.

Golding resigned as Prime Minister in 2011 and was succeeded by Andrew Holness as the leader of the JLP and Prime Minister of Jamaica. Golding retired from politics in 2012.

Portia Simpson Miller, ON, M.P.

Portia Simpson Miller, or 'Madam P", as she is affectionately called, is the first and only female Prime Minister of Jamaica to date. She was born on December 12, 1945, in Wood Hall, Jamaica and began her political career as a member of the People's National Party (PNP) in the 1970s.

In 2006, Simpson Miller was elected as the President of the PNP, and in 2007, she became the Prime Minister of Jamaica, serving until 2011. During her tenure as Prime Minister, she implemented several important policy initiatives, including the Jamaica Emergency Employment Program, which aimed to provide jobs and economic opportunities for Jamaican citizens.

Simpson Miller was also an advocate for gender equality and social justice, and her policies and programs aimed to improve the lives of marginalized and vulnerable communities in Jamaica. In addition to her political career, she has been involved in various philanthropic efforts, including supporting education and health initiatives in Jamaica.

Simpson Miller retired from politics in 2020, but her legacy as a trailblazer and champion for social justice in Jamaica continues to inspire new generations of Jamaicans.

Portia Simpson Miller wore several hats locally and overseas, including, but not limited to:

- Member of the Council of Women World Leaders.
- Member of the Board of Trustees of CIFAL in Atlanta Georgia.
- Chairperson of the Caribbean Forum of Ministers responsible for decentralization, local government, community development and citizen participation, and also board member of the Commonwealth Local Government forum.
- Vice president of the Organization of American States' High-level Inter-American Network on Decentralization, Local Government and Citizen Participation

The former Prime Minister was a very avid and active supporter of the Peoples National party (P.N.P) for several years prior to her ascension to office and is still considered as one of the stalwarts of the party.

Andrew Michael Holness, ON, PC, MP

Andrew Michael Holness, Jamaica's ninth Prime Minister, was born on July 22, 1972, in Spanish Town, Jamaica. He entered the record books as one of the Prime Ministers who served the shortest term in office when he governed the country from October 2011 to January 2012. Holness began his political career as a member of the Jamaica Labour Party (JLP). He was first elected to the Jamaican Parliament in 1997 to represent the West Central St. Andrew constituency. He served in various positions, including Minister of Education and Minister of Housing, before being elected as the leader of the JLP in 2011.

In the 2011 general election, Holness led the JLP to a narrow victory, becoming the youngest person ever to be elected as Prime Minister of Jamaica at the age of 39. However, the JLP was defeated in the 2012 election, and Holness became the Leader of the Opposition. Holness led the JLP to victory again in the 2016 general election, and he was again sworn in as Prime Minister on March 3, 2016. He was re-elected in the 2020 general election, and he continues to serve as the Prime Minister of Jamaica.

During his tenure as Prime Minister, Holness has focused on economic growth, job creation, and social development. He has implemented several initiatives aimed at improving the lives of Jamaican citizens, including the HOPE Program, which provides skills training and employment opportunities for young people; and the National Identification System (NIDS), which aims to establish a secure and reliable system for identifying Jamaican citizens. He is married and has two sons, Adam and Matthew.

The transformation of the economy and the ultimate goal of transforming the country and the economy into an exemplary international destination once more remains a work in progress. Jamaica, once considered 'The Pearl of the Caribbean", still remains a prime tourist destination, and it is the desire of all Jamaicans to restore it to its former glory.

PART 2
ELEMENTS OF JAMAICA'S GREATNESS

What Makes Jamaica Great

CHAPTER 5
Reggae Music and Reggae Ambassadors

S inging, dancing, folklore and drama are just some of the ways that groups of people entertain themselves. The Africans, once removed from their homeland, were no exception, so the descendants continued to embrace these traditions; and out of this transition came Mento, Ska, Rock Steady, Reggae, and eventually dancehall. There are some iconic names of groups and individuals who came out of this Jamaican music revolution and evolution; and although we may not be able to highlight in detail their full contribution to our greatness, the names will be listed and you can do your own research on them.

Jamaica has enjoyed an extremely rich heritage in the creation and proliferation of music that has made a valuable contribution to the music industry both locally and internationally. As a country, Jamaica has produced many music ambassadors; of note is Harry Belafonte. Although not a Reggae ambassador, he was of Jamaican descent and made history by becoming the first individual recording artiste to have an album that sold over one million copies. Belafonte passed away in May 2023. He never forgot his Jamaican roots and is testament of the greatness of our people.

Some of the early pioneers of our musical evolution were: The Upsetters, The Ethiopians, Derrick Morgan, The Pioneers, and Clancy Eccles. In the 1940's and 1950's, we had Mento, in the 1960's we transcended to Ska, and by 1978, Reggae had taken its place as a musical representation of our culture. We may not all agree that the giants mentioned in this synopsis are the most outstanding, but history will support the fact that the impact they have made in the proliferation of Brand Jamaica, and reggae music, is quite material.

We are a people who have endured and still continue to have challenges on our journey to garner the well-earned place we have carved out as our niche in the world. There are so many contributors who deserve merit for their input in this ongoing struggle. In the music industry, there are many stalwarts who may have not been given exclusive mention in this production. It is not that their contributions have not been noteworthy. However, our history has been enhanced by so much greatness that in this volume, we can only showcase some of who we are.

Reggae music has played a significant role in the development of the Jamaican people. It is noteworthy that a little island with a population in excess of 2.7 million people has produced so many giants in a variety of musical genres. Locally, and internationally, we cannot accurately measure the impact that Reggae music has had overall, but mention has been made below of some of the positives.

Cultural identity: Reggae music has become a symbol of Jamaica's cultural identity, both at home and abroad. The music reflects the unique history and experiences of the Jamaican people, and has helped to establish a sense of pride and identity among Jamaicans.

Social commentary: Reggae music has been used as a platform for social commentary and political activism. Many reggae songs address issues such as poverty, inequality, oppression, crime, and corruption, and have helped to raise awareness and inspire action among the Jamaican people.

Economic development: The popularity of reggae music has also contributed to Jamaica's economic development, through tourism and the export of Jamaican music and culture. Reggae music has helped to establish Jamaica as a cultural and artistic hub, attracting visitors and generating revenue for the country. Artists such as Bob Marley, Dennis Brown Sean Paul, Beenie Man, Beres Hammond and many other artistes are household names internationally.

Community building: Reggae music has been used as a tool for community building and social cohesion. Many reggae concerts and festivals bring together people from different backgrounds and communities, fostering a sense of unity and togetherness.

Educational opportunities: Reggae music has also provided educational opportunities for the Jamaican people, through music programs and schools. Many young people in Jamaica have learned to play instruments and have performed reggae music, providing them with skills and opportunities for personal and professional development.

Reggae music has played and continues to play a significant role in the development of the Jamaican people, both in terms of cultural identity and social and economic development of the Jamaican people, both in terms of cultural identity and social and economic development. Its impact on the country and its people continues to be celebrated and recognized around the world.

Reggae Ambassadors

The name Bob Marley is synonymous with Jamaica. Prior to the rise of Usain Bolt, the fastest man alive, the international appreciation of Bob Marley's music helped people identify Jamaica. Bob Marley is the most iconic musician in the Hall of Fame for the proliferation of Reggae across the globe and his legacy is being committed to memory by his children, and grandchildren.

Being the creator of Reggae, Jamaica has established awareness of the popular genre and that legacy will be handed down for generations to come. The term "Reggae Ambassadors of Jamaica" refers to a group of musicians who have played a major role in popularizing Jamaican reggae music around the world. Bob Marley and the Wailers are among the most prominent reggae ambassadors of Jamaica, and we have singled them out by providing a brief profile of the history of their development and their achievements.

Bob Marley and the Wailers was a Jamaican Reggae group that was formed in the 1960s. The original line-up included Bob Marley, Peter Tosh, and Bunny Livingston, (nicknamed Bunny Wailer), who were childhood friends and shared a passion for music. The Wailers were known for their unique sound, which blended elements of reggae, ska, and rock music. They gained popularity in Jamaica and soon began to attract attention from music producers and record labels around the world.

In the 1970s, Bob Marley and the Wailers became one of the most influential and successful Reggae groups of all time, with hit songs such as "No Woman No Cry , "Trench Town Rock", " "Get Up, Stand Up" and "One Love." Their music was known for its socially conscious themes, which reflected the political and social issues facing Jamaica and the world at the time.

Marley and the Wailers were also known for their powerful live performances, and they toured extensively throughout the world, spreading the message of Reggae music to new audiences. The main back –up singers that supported The Wailers, then, were The I-Threes, which comprised Judy Mowatt, Rita Marley, and Marcia Griffiths.

After Bob Marley's untimely death in 1981, the Wailers continued to perform and record music, with various members of the group taking on new roles and responsibilities. Today, the music of Bob Marley and the Wailers continues to be celebrated and honoured around the world and their legacy as pioneers of reggae music lives on.

Eventually when the band was dissolved, Bob continued his legendary journey alone, building an empire, and leaving the legacy he has now created. The children and grandchildren of the reggae legend (including Ziggy, Stephen, Damion, KyMani, and most recently Julian and Skip) continue to make waves in the music fraternity.

Besides Bob Marley, the list of Reggae greats, including those in the Roots Rock Reggae brotherhood, are too numerous to mention, and every one of these icons have stamped their authority and etched their trademarks on the Reggae Hall of Fame. Some of the most popular ones include: Jimmy Cliff, Toots and the Maytals, Burning Spear, Dennis Brown (The Crown Prince of Reggae), Gregory Isaacs, Sugar Minott, Ken Boothe, Cynthia Schloss, John Holt, Eric Donaldson, Freddy McGreggor, Alton Ellis, Beres Hammond, Ernie Smith, Bob Andy, Marcia Griffiths, Burning Spear, and Third World.

Dancehall Music

The genre of music popularly known as "Dancehall" evolved in the late 70's and has morphed from several different strains of Jamaican musical origins, namely Ska, Reggae, Rocksteady, and Dub. It is not possible to give detailed commentary on all the champions who popularized this genre, but we can mention some and laud them for their valuable contributions to our musical journey. Artists such as: Shabba Ranks, Shaggy "(Mr.

Bombastic)," Sean Paul, Beenie Man, Bounty Killer, Buju Banton, Spice, Vybz Kartel, Alkaline, Popcaan , Elephant Man, Mavado, Busy Signal, Koshens, Mr. Vegas, Lady Saw (now Minister Marion Hall) Capleton, Yellowman, Ninjaman, Tami Chynn, Tessanne Chin, Maxi Priest and many others.

If you were to read the biographies of each of these Reggae ambassadors, you will not only see their outstanding achievements but also that characteristic ability of Jamaicans to pull themselves up by their bootstraps, rise from the ashes, and excel in the global community.

An old Jamaican adage commonly used is " wi likkle , but wi tallawah", which simply means, do not be fooled by the fact that we are only approximately three million people, because we have put ourselves in a position on the world stage to let our voices be heard. Literally, and figuratively our musicians have made their voices heard. We salute them for their contributions to the greatness of our island paradise.

CHAPTER 6
Kings & Queens of Comedy and Drama

The arts have played a significant role in the development of Jamaican people and culture. From music to dance, visual arts, literature and theatre, the arts have contributed to shaping the Jamaican identity and have helped to express and celebrate the country's unique cultural heritage.

The visual arts have played a significant role in Jamaica's development. Artists like Edna Manley and Albert Huie have used their work to depict Jamaican life and culture, capturing the essence of the country's people, landscapes and history. Their work has helped to preserve Jamaica's cultural heritage and promote it to the world.

In addition, theatre and dance have contributed to the development of the Jamaican people, providing a space for expression and creativity. Louise Bennett, Charles Hyatt, Ranny Williams, Oliver Samuels, Leonie Forbes, Fae Ellington, and many others have made their impact on the arts by their individual and collective contributions. The National Dance Theatre Company of Jamaica, for example, has been instrumental in promoting Jamaican dance forms like traditional folk dance and the popular dancehall style.

Without a doubt, the arts have provided a means for Jamaican people to express themselves, preserve their cultural heritage and promote their identity and achievements to the world. The arts have also contributed to the country's economy, with music, in particular, being a significant export and contributing to Jamaica's reputation as a creative and dynamic nation.

The Correlation between the Arts and Slavery

There is a correlation between slavery and the arts in Jamaica. The legacy of slavery and colonialism has had a profound impact on the development of Jamaican art, music, dance, and other forms of cultural expression.

During the era of slavery, African slaves in Jamaica were forbidden from practicing their cultural traditions and were forced to adopt the customs and practices of their European captors. However, despite these restrictions, enslaved Africans found ways to preserve their cultural heritage through music, dance, storytelling and other forms of expression. They created and enacted their own forms of entertainment in their private moments, and tried to somehow retain their legacy which had been tainted by slavery, having been stolen from their families and their homeland.

One of the most significant contributions of enslaved Africans to Jamaican culture was the development of traditional Jamaican music, including mento, ska, reggae, and dancehall.

These musical styles were heavily influenced by African rhythms and traditions, and they played an essential role in the cultural and social life of Jamaica.

The legacy of slavery also influenced the development of Jamaican visual art, literature and theatre. Many Jamaican artists, writers, and playwrights have explored the themes of slavery, oppression and resistance in their work, drawing on the experiences of their ancestors to create powerful and insightful works of art. This legacy has indeed had a profound impact on the development of the arts in Jamaica. Despite the historical injustices faced by enslaved Africans, their cultural traditions and expressions have endured, shaping and enriching the vibrant and diverse cultural landscape of modern-day Jamaica.

Although there are many Jamaican cultural icons, the name Louise Bennett Coverly has become synonymous with Jamaican culture. In terms of comedy and theatre, Oliver Samuels is the most renowned Jamaican entertainer. In this section, we will pay homage to them and highlight other kings and queens of Jamaican drama and comedy.

Louise Bennett Coverley, OM, OJ

(c) 1989 The Gleaner Co. (Media) Ltd.

"My Auntie Roachy sey," Louise Simone Bennett-Coverly, OM, OJ, MBE, or Miss Lou as she was affectionately called, was a storyteller, a teacher of culture, a comedian, a writer of poems and dialects and a cultural icon whose contribution remains unequalled to this very day. Known for her stories of 'Aunty Roachy", and Bredda Anancy, she has been loved and revered by Jamaicans, at home, and abroad.

Born on September 7th, 1919, Miss Lou, wrote her first dialect poem when she was fourteen years old and subsequently obtained a British Council Scholarship which saw her attending the Royal Academy of Dramatic Art. She taught drama at The Extra Mural Department of the University of the West Indies, and also lectured on music and Jamaican folklore both in The United Kingdom and the United States.

Miss Lou's outstanding contributions earned her numerous accolades, including, but not limited to:

- The Order of Jamaica -1974
- The Norman Manley Award for Excellence (Field of Arts)
- M.B.E.
- The Institute of Jamaica's Musgrave Gold and Silver Medals in the fields of Arts and Culture

- The Honorary Degree of Doctor of Letters from the University of the West Indies
- The Honorary Degree of Doctor of Letters from York University in Toronto, Canada.

Miss Lou's influence on folklore, drama, and the awareness of the profound impact of our dialect and our history, has made her a household name for all Jamaicans, locally, and in the Diaspora. She made her final departure from this stage of life on July 26th, 2006. She will be forever in our hearts, and we can only echo her own words and wishes, by asking her to "Walk Good".

Oliver Samuels, OD [The King of Comedy]:

If ever there was a title most aptly bestowed on an individual, it would be the one given to Oliver Samuels for his contribution to the arts, with specific accolades for acting, especially in the field of comedy. He is known as "The King of Comedy", a title which he has earned over and over. Oliver is one of those persons who has the propensity to make people laugh by just looking at him.

Mi know him wi vex if mi tell people sey him middle name is Adolphus, but Oliver Adolphus Samuels was born in St. Mary,

Jamaica, on November 4th, 1948. After a challenging start to his acting career, Oliver's gradual rise to stardom was enhanced by his performances in the country's pantomimes for which he got recognition. He has played roles in movies and television productions, at home, and abroad, but there is none that has cemented his legacy in the minds and the hearts of the Jamaican people like the series "Oliver at Large".

Jamaica, our little island, of barely a handful of people when compared to the population on the world stage, has produced so many giants that it is phenomenal. Oliver Samuels is another treasure that we have introduced to the world who has carved out his own niche. Big up Oliver, wi proud a yu.

Nationally Recognized Contributors

These men and women have been recognized by the government of Jamaica for their outstanding contributions to the Jamaica entertainment industry. They have been conferred with national honours such as the Order of Distinction (OD) or the Order of Jamaica (OJ). They include:

- **Ranny Williams,** who was born on October 26, 1912, and made his transition on August 11th, 1980. In recognition of his contributions to Jamaican culture, the Ranny Williams Entertainment Centre in Kingston was named in his honor. The centre hosts a range of cultural events, including theatre productions, concerts and comedy shows; and serves as a hub for Jamaica's vibrant entertainment industry.

- **Volier "Maffie" Johnson,** was born December 14th, 1951 and made his transition on July 9th, 2021. There are, however, some sources that indicate that his actual date of birth was December 16th, 1951. "Maffie" was one of the early forerunners of Jamaica's entertainment industry. The Jamaican government bestowed the country's sixth largest honour on him in 2013, the Order of Distinction for his contribution to theatre.

- **Leonie Forbes, OD:** Mrs. Leonie Forbes-Amiel had an exemplary career in broadcasting, television and drama; and her contribution to the Arts, and the areas in which she excelled can only be described as "Par Excellence." She received several honours and awards including: Silver Musgrave Medal, Order of Distinction of Jamaica, (Officer Class), 1980, Centenary Medal, Bronze Musgrave Medal (1973) and "My Life in the Theatre" medal by the Mexican Theatre of Latin America and the Caribbean (2001).

- **Joan Andrea Hutchinson,** OD: Storyteller, writer, broadcaster, actress, motivational speaker and teacher. She has made considerable contributions in the realms of Jamaican Culture and has been considered by many as the next Miss Lou (Louise Bennett). In an effort to embrace her culture, she once had her hair done in "Chiney Bumps", and received the ire of persons who could not identify with their natural heritage and considered it demeaning. That position has since changed, somewhat, as Jamaicans are now becoming more aware of the need to embrace their origins and culture. Some of her popular works include the poem: "Dat Bumpyhead Gal," her renditions of *Uriah Preach, No Lickle Twang, Mout - Amassi, Dutty Tough,* and *Bun an Cheese.*

* **Charles Hyatt, OD** [Feb. 14, 1927 – Oct. 7, 2007]: Charles Hyatt, Order of Distinction (OD), was a Jamaican actor, director, and playwright. Hyatt was also a well-known actor in Jamaican film and television. He appeared in several Jamaican films, including "The Harder They Come" (1972) and "No Place like Home" (2006). Hyatt was known for his commitment to Jamaican culture and his contributions to the development of the country's entertainment industry. In recognition of his contributions, he was posthumously awarded the Order of Jamaica, one of the country's highest honours, in 2008. Hyatt was awarded the Institute of Jamaica Centenary Medal, the Silver Musgrave Medal and the Best Actor Award in 1958-1959, and 1966-1967.

* **Glen "Titus" Campbell, Order of Distinction, OD,** is a Jamaican actor and comedian and he is not to be confused with the American musician Glen Campbell. Glen has appeared in several Jamaican films and television shows, including "Third World Cop" (1999), "One Love" (2003), and "The Itch" (2010). He is also known for his role as "Bentley" in the popular Jamaican television series "Royal Palm Estate," which aired from 1993 to 2008. Glen Campbell has also acted in productions with Oliver Samuels and other notable entertainers such as in the production" Cutie & The Freak".

- **Fae Ellington** is a Lecturer and Media personality, actress, radio and television broadcaster who has also been a recipient of the Order of Distinction Commander Class. Fae has taught Broadcast Announcing and Presentation at the Caribbean School of Media and Communication at the University of the West Indies since 1985, and was a foundation member of the Jamaica School of Drama. Her awards and recognitions include: Order of Distinction (Officer Class, 1998); Best Director nomination, Actor Boy Awards for "Who will Sing for Lena" (2005); Order of Distinction (Commander Class, 2015)

Notable Mentions

Although these actors/comedians have not yet received national honors, their contribution to the industry at the time of writing has been well recognized. These include: Owen 'Blakka' Ellis, Christopher Johnny Daley, Alton H. Hardware as Fancy Cat, and Ian M. Ellis, popularly known as Ity, (in the production Ity & Fancy Cat), and Keith 'Shebada" Ramsey.

CHAPTER 7

Our Athletic Ambassadors

Sports has been a significant part of Caribbean culture, shaping and influencing the region's people in various ways. Primarily, it may have emanated from the need to provide our own entertainment after we were taken from our homeland and brought to a strange place, or possibly having to find ways to outrun our captors when we escaped captivity. Whatever the circumstances, we have been given the opportunity to display our athletic acumen on the world stage, and we have done so, in a most outstanding fashion. Here are some ways in which sports has contributed to the development and shaping of Caribbean people:

National Pride and Identity: Sports has played a significant role in developing national pride and identity in the Caribbean. When the West Indies cricket team won its first Test match in 1950, it was a significant moment for the region and it helped to unite Caribbean people from different countries. The success of the team continued in the following decades, creating a sense of national pride and identity.

Social Cohesion: Sports has the ability to bring people together, creating social cohesion and promoting unity. Sporting events, such as cricket matches, football games, and athletic competitions, provide opportunities for people to gather and share a common experience.

Economic Development: Sports has the potential to drive economic development in the Caribbean. International sporting events, such as the Cricket World Cup, have brought significant revenue to the region through tourism and other industries.

Health and Wellness: Participating in sports is essential for maintaining good health and wellness. The Caribbean has a high prevalence of non-communicable diseases, such as diabetes and heart disease. Promoting and encouraging participation in sports can help to reduce the incidences of these diseases and improve the overall health of the population.

Role Models: Sports provides opportunities for Caribbean people to become role models and inspire others. Many Caribbean athletes have achieved great success in their respective sports and have become heroes and role models for young people.

In summary, sports has played a vital role in shaping the Caribbean people by creating national pride and identity, promoting social cohesion, driving economic development, improving health and wellness, and providing role models for young people.

Track and field in Jamaica has its roots in the early 20th century, when the first track and field meets were held on the island. Many of the early athletes who competed in these meets were former slaves or the descendants of the enslaved, and they saw sports as a way to break free from the poverty and oppression that had characterized their lives. Yes, there is a correlation between sports and slavery in the Caribbean. The history of sports in the Caribbean is closely tied to the legacy of slavery and colonialism in the region.

Today, many of the most successful Caribbean athletes are descendants of enslaved Africans who were forced to work on plantations. These athletes have overcome historical and social barriers to achieve success in their respective sports, inspiring others and demonstrating the resilience and determination of Caribbean people in the face of adversity.

Despite the historical injustices faced by Caribbean people, sports have become a source of pride, inspiration and achievement for many. Jamaica has a rich history of producing world-class track and field athletes who have become ambassadors for the country and its culture. These athletes have brought great pride to Jamaica and have helped to showcase the country's talent and resilience on the international stage. Over the years, our athletes have made exemplary inroads in the storybooks by being forces to be reckoned with in both group and individual events, and in both male and female categories. Whether it is, Penn Relays, World Championships, Olympics or Diamond leagues, our presence is always noticeable. Jamaican athletes continue to excel in track, and field, with many athletes from the island winning medals at the Olympic Games and other international competitions. Today, Jamaica is widely regarded as a world leader in track and field, and its athletes are among the most successful and celebrated in the sport.

The success of Jamaican athletes in this sport is a testament to the resilience, determination and talent of the people of Jamaica. In this section we will highlight some of our iconic athletes who have brought great renown to Jamaica. A brief profile has been provided for some of the most notable figures. These athletes and many others like them, have helped to shape Jamaica's global image and have inspired generations of Jamaican youth to pursue excellence in athletics and beyond. They are true ambassadors for the country and serve as powerful symbols of Jamaican talent, pride, and resilience.

Snapshots of Jamaica's Track and Field Ambassadors

Three most important forerunners in the history of Jamaican track and field are Arthur Wint, Herb McKinley and Donald Quarrie. Here is a brief snapshot of their lives and achievements.

Arthur Wint, OD, MBE

Arthur Stanley Wint OD MBE (25 May 1920 – 19 October 1992, won Jamaica's first Olympic gold medal in the 400 metres (46.2 seconds), at the London Games, beating his teammate Herb McKenley. Wint was a former soldier and had served in World War II as a Royal Air Force (RAF) pilot; and his success on the track helped to inspire a generation of Jamaican athletes. He later became a physician and High Commissioner to the United Kingdom.

He competed at the 1948 and 1952 Olympics, whilst a medical student at St Bartholomew's

Hospital, London. He won two gold and two silver medals, becoming the first Jamaican Olympic gold medalist. In the 800 metres he won silver, after American Mal Whitfield's gold. Wint missed a probable third medal when he pulled a muscle in the 4 × 400 metres relay final.

Herb McKenley, OM

Herb McKenley was a Jamaican track and field athlete who is widely regarded as one of Jamaica's greatest ever athletes. Born in 1922 in Clarendon, Jamaica, Mc-Kenley was a middle-distance runner who competed in the 1948, 1952, and 1956 Olympics, winning a total of four medals.

McKenley was a key member of the Jamaican relay teams that won gold in the 4x400m relay at the 1952 Helsinki Olympics and the 4x100m relay at the 1956 Melbourne Olympics. He also won silver in the 100m and 400m events at the 1948 London Olympics.

In addition to his Olympic success, McKenley set several world records during his career, including the 400m and 4x440 yard relay. He was also a successful coach, leading Jamaica's national track and field team in the 1960s and 1970s.

Today, McKenley is remembered as a true legend of Jamaican athletics and a trailblazer for future generations of Jamaican athletes. His impact on the sport and on Jamaican society as a whole is immeasurable and his legacy continues to inspire and motivate young Jamaicans to pursue excellence in athletics and beyond.

Donald Quarrie, OJ

Donald Quarrie is a former Jamaican track and field athlete who was born on February 25, 1951, in Kingston, Jamaica. He is considered one of Jamaica's greatest sprinters and is also known for his contributions to Jamaican athletics as a coach and administrator.

Quarrie first came to international attention as a teenager when he competed in the 1968 Olympic Games in Mexico City, where he finished fifth in the 200 m. He went on to win a gold medal in the 200m and a silver medal in the 100m at the 1976 Montreal Olympics, as well as a bronze medal in the 200m at the 1980 Moscow Olympics. In addition to his Olympics success, Quarrie also won several medals at the Commonwealth Games and the Pan American Games.

After retiring from competition, Quarrie became a coach and administrator, serving as the technical director for the Jamaican Track and Field team and as the president of the Jamaica Athletics Administrative Association. He also founded the Donald Quarrie High-Performance Training Centre in Jamaica, which is dedicated to developing young Jamaican athletes and helping them to achieve their full potential.

Quarrie has been recognized for his contributions to Jamaican athletics and was awarded the Order of Jamaica in 2009. He is also a member of the Jamaica Sports Hall of Fame and the International Association of Athletics Federations Hall of Fame. In order to commit his memory to the legendary status it deserves, the Donald Quarrie High School was named in his honour.

In recent history, 2008 – 2022, the names like Usain Bolt, Shelly-Ann Fraser-Pryce and Elaine Thompson-Herah have cemented our standing as the sprint capital of the world. These three, at the time of writing, remain the fastest male and female track and field athletes in the world. Here is a brief profile of these track and field stars.

Usain St. Leo Bolt OJ, CD, OLY (The Legend)

The Honourable Usain Bolt, OJ, CD, the Lightning Bolt, the legend, the greatest sprinter of all times was born to Wellesley and Jennifer Bolt in Sherwood Content Jamaica on August 21st, 1986. Bolt has transformed and brought the sport back from a place where doping scandals had undermined the credibility of the athletes and had the sporting community questioning the future of the sport.

Bolt is now retired but he is still widely regarded as one of the greatest sprinters in history, known for his incredible speed, power, and charisma. Bolt first came to international attention in the mid-2000s, when he set several world junior records in the 200m and 4x100m relay. He went on to win numerous major international competitions during his career, including eight Olympic gold medals, 11 World Championship gold medals and two Commonwealth Games gold medals.

Bolt is best known for his performances in the 100m and 200m, in which he set multiple world records and became the first person in history to hold world records in both events at the same time.

Bolt is the current World Record holder in the 100 and 200m, and also the 4x100 relay. Below is a summary, though not exhaustive list of his crowning glory and accolades:

- Only sprinter to win 100 and 200 metre titles in three consecutive Olympics, namely, 2008, 2012 and 2016.
- Only person to hold both the 100 and 200m records since "fully automatic time" became mandatory, which he did in the 2008 Beijing Olympics.
- Eight-time Olympic gold medal winner.
- Eleven-time World Champion, who won consecutive gold medals in the 100m, 200m, 4x100 relays from 2009 to 2015. He lost the 100m in 2011 due to a false start.
- Only athlete to hold three titles in both the 100 and 200m at the World Championship.
- World under 20 and under 18 records for the 200m
- IAAF World Athlete of the Year.
- Track & Field Athlete of the Year.
- Laureus World Sportsman of the Year.
- The IAAF men's Athlete of the Year Award in Monaco.

This 6'5" giant of a man and a champion of champions has left footprints in the Athletic Hall of Fame that will not be easily filled any time soon.

Shelly Ann Fraser-Pryce, OD, OJ

Shelly-Ann Fraser-Pryce nick-named, and affectionately called "The Pocket Rocket" because of her remarkable speed for such a small and petite athlete, was born in Kingston, Jamaica on December 27, 1986. She is widely considered one of the greatest female sprinters of all time.

Fraser-Pryce first gained inter-national attention in 2008, when she won her first Olympic gold medal in the 100m at the Beijing Olympics. She went on to win gold in the 100m again at the 2012 London Olympics, and the 2016 Rio Olympics, becoming the first woman in history to win three Olympic gold medals in the 100 meters.

Fraser-Pryce has also had great success at the World Championships, winning gold in the 100m in 2009, 2013, 2015, and 2019, and in the 4x100m relay in 2013 and 2015. She has set multiple world records and is known for her explosive starts and powerful finishing kick.

Fraser-Pryce's legacy as one of the greatest sprinters in Jamaican history is secure, and she continues to inspire and motivate young athletes in Jamaica and around the world.

The "Pocket Rocket" defended her 100m title in the Olympic Games of 2012, thereby writing in the history books by becoming the third woman to win successive gold medals at the Games. She further went on to win the 100m in the Diamond League in Lausanne, Switzerland, on August 26th, in a time of 10.60, making her the third fastest woman in the history of the event.

Elaine Thompson-Herah, OD

Elaine Thompson-Herah is a Jamaican athlete who specializes in the 100 and 200m, and also contributes in the 4x100 relays. She was born on June 28, 1992, in the parish of Manchester, Jamaica, and is widely considered one of the greatest female sprinters in history.

Over her career she attained 9 gold medals, 3 silver medals and 2 bronze medals in World champion-ships, Pan American Games, Common-wealth games, Diamond League, World Champion-ships and Olympic Games. These performances were in the 100M, 200M, 4x100M, 4x200M relays, and a 60m event.

Elaine has transcended the realm of outstanding feats in her achievement of being the only woman in history to have defended both the 100 and 200m titles in two successive Olympic games, namely in 2016, and more recently in Tokyo in 2021. This remarkable performance has only been equalled by her fellow countryman, and the greatest sprinter to have ever lived, Usain St. Leo Bolt.

Thompson-Herah continued her success at the 2019 World Championships, where she won gold in the 100m, 200m, and 4x100m relay, becoming the first woman to win the "sprint triple" at a major international competition since Griffith-Joyner in 1988.

She was awarded the Order of Distinction in 2016 for her contributions to Jamaican athletics. To compound these outstanding accolades, Elaine went further in the Tokyo Olympics to secure another gold medal as part of the Jamaican relay team that won the 4x100 relay. She has really proven herself to be an exceptional sprinter, and one of the all-time greats. In the Diamond League, Prefontaine Classics in Eugene, in 2021, Elaine recorded the second fastest time ever in this event, a whopping 10.54 seconds. This was only bested by Florence Griffiths Joyner and Elaine appears to be poised to put that record in her rear-view mirror. Only time will tell, so let's watch and see. In 2021, a world leading time of 10.54 has put the world on notice, so in the ensuing years, we are hoping she continues to take her craft to a whole different level. Well done, Elaine, Well done.!

Another signature achievement by the Jamaican men and women on the international stage has been their dramatic wins in 4x400m relays for men and women in the last two decades. Both the Jamaican men and women's 4x100 relay teams have set World and Olympic records in their respective events. The younger generation of athletes are also poised to keep Jamaica's record intact. It is worthy of note today that in the history of the men's 100, 200m and 4x100relays, Jamaica has representation in the top ten best times which is unprecedented and bears admirable recognition. See page 70 of the Top 10 Historical World 100 and 200m rankings by Peterson Larsoon (2023).

Historical World 100m Rankings (Men):

1.	Usain Bolt	(Jamaica)	9.58
2.	Usain Bolt	(Jamaica)	9.63
3.	Usain Bolt	(Jamaica)	9.69
4.	Tyson Gay	(U.S.A)	9.69
5.	Yohan Blake	(Jamaica)	9.69.
6.	Tyson Gay	(U.S.A)	9.71
7.	Usain Bolt	(Jamaica)	9.72
8.	Asafa Powell	(Jamaica)	9.72
9.	Asafa Powell	(Jamaica)	9.74
10.	Justin Gatlin	(U.S.A)	9.74

Historical World 200 m ranking (Men)

1.	Usain Bolt	(Jamaica)	19.19
2.	Yohan Blake	(Jamaica)	19.26
3.	Usain Bolt	(Jamaica)	19.30
4.	Noah Lyles	(USA)	19.31
5.	Michael Johnson	(U.S.A)	19.32
6.	Usain Bolt	(Jamaica)	19.32
7.	Usain Bolt	(Jamaica)	19.40
8.	Yohan Blake	(Jamaica)	19.44
9.	Noah Lyles	(USA)	19.46
10.	Erriyon Knighton	(USA)	19.49

Other Notable Track and Field Ambassadors

We could not close this section without mentioning some of the other notable Track and Field Ambassadors who have won World and Olympic Medals including Asafa Powell, Veronica Campbell-Brown, Merlene Ottey, Grace Jackson, Juliet Cuthbert, Deon Hemmings, Kerron Stewart, Sherone Simpson, Shereefa Lloyd, Sherika Williams, Yohan Blake, Warren Weir, Hansel

Parchment, Omar McLeod, Michael Frater, Bridgette Foster–Hylton, Melanie Walker, Shericka Jackson, Briana Williams, and Megan Tapper.

Special mention must be given to Asafa Powell who dominated the 100m sprints prior to the legendary Usain Bolt, and notably the athlete who has broken the ten-second barrier more than anyone else—97 times. He holds (at the time of writing) the world record for the 100-yard dash with a time of 9.09.

Greatness Beyond Track and Field

Although Track and Field has been the most popular field where Jamaica has shone, the greatness of our people extends to other sporting areas such as cricket, swimming, and football. Some of the most renown names in these fields are:

- **Cricket**: George Headley, Michael Holding, Courtney Walsh, Jimmy Adams, Jeffrey Dujon and Christopher Gayle.

- **Football [The Reggae Boyz]:** In 1998, the Jamaican Reggae Boyz became a national treasure when they qualified for the 1998 FIFA World Cup. They were also winners of the Caribbean Cup on five different occasions.

- **Swimming:** The name Alia Atkinson easily stands out as our most accomplished swimmer on the world stage.

- **BobSleigh**: In a country where snow doesn't fall, it is indeed an outstanding feat to have a team that can perform in a BobSleigh competition. This is what the Jamaican team did in their debut in the 1988 Winter Olympics in Calgary, Alberta, Canada. Since then, we have had a two-man team in the 1992, 1994, 1998, 2002, and 2014 Winter Olympics. Their success was immortalized in the popular movie "Cool Runnings."

Over the years, the success of Jamaican athletes in sports is a testament to the resilience, determination and talent of the people of Jamaica. This is definitely an area where the greatness of our people is unquestioned.

CHAPTER 8

Business Moguls Local and Overseas

Jamaica's business communities and our achievements in business are reflections of the greatness of our people. Some people will resign themselves to their fate; while others will rise and soar like eagles so that the world may see their achievements and appreciate the journey it took to get them there. Most of the business moguls mentioned in this book rose from humble beginnings and through blood, sweat and tears, have gained international recognition for their success. We recognize their resilience and accomplishments. The people mentioned in this chapter are only a snapshot of great Jamaican entrepreneurs and do not in any way cover the full entrepreneurial landscape representative of Jamaica's business communities and our achievements. They have been selected only to give a feel of our achievements by highlighting some of the prominent names that have gained, and still hold international recognition.

These individuals possess the grit and substance from which all Jamaicans are made. They, along with others mentioned in previous chapters, embody the qualities toward which all Jamaicans can aspire and can achieve if they embrace the greatness within themselves. Their success is a lesson, an inspiration, and a goal for those who have not yet achieved their greatness but who aspire to do so.

In August 2014, an article in the Jamaica Gleaner listed 10 of Jamaica's most outstanding business giants. The list showcased:

1. **Don Wehby**, Chief Executive Officer of Grace Kennedy.

2. **Earl Jarrett** General Manager of Jamaica National Building Society (JNBS) since October 1999.

3. **Donna Duncan-Scott**, Managing Director of Jamaica Money Market Brokers Ltd since 1998.

4. **Jacqueline Sharp**, President and Chief Executive officer of Scotiabank

5. **Audrey Hinchcliffe,** head of Manpower and Maintenance Services Ltd.

6. **Karl Hendrickson,** founder of the National baking empire

7. **Phillip Gore,** Executive chairman of Gore Developments

8. **Glen Christian,** Chairman and founder of Cari-Med and Kirk Distributors

9. **Basil Johnson,** Founder and Managing Director of Montego Bay-based Discount Lumber & Hardware Limited, Discount Lumber Limited, and Discount Mart Limited.

10. **Fred Smith,** Managing director of Tropical Tours and Exclusive Holidays Limited

Notwithstanding the presentation of this list, some of the more renowned business moguls were not mentioned. Names such as Michael Lee Chin, the late Gordon "Butch" Stewart, Joseph Matalon, Joseph John Issa, Lascelles Chin, Chris Blackwell, Blossom O' Meally-Nelson, Paula Kerr-Jarrett and Wayne Chen, Marlene Gray, Marcia Forbes, Dr. Kingsley Chin, Joan Webley, and Kingsley Cooper were omitted from this listing.

For inspiration, we have chosen to capture the profiles of some of these moguls, namely Michael Lee Chin, Gordon Butch Stewart, Audrey Hinchcliffe, Phillip Gore and Glen Christian. For more inspiration, you can also research the names of the entrepreneurs previously mentioned.

Gordon "Butch" Stewart

The name Gordon "Butch" Stewart is a name that resonates in the hearts of the Jamaican people as a memoir of what can be achieved by sheer determination and steadfastness. The journey from Appliance Traders, to Sandals, to Beaches has been a memorable one that has contributed significantly to the showcasing of Jamaican life, culture and hospitality all over the world.

Butch's exposure to business began when he helped his mother in her personal business until he started as an appliance trader before he turned 17. He later started Appliance Traders Limited (ATL) with a second-hand car, a second-hand pick-up and a rented office. ATL now owns the Jamaica Observer Newspaper and ATL Group are the distributors for Honda Motor Cars in Jamaica.

Sometime between the 1970's and 1090's, Butch bought two old run down hotels and made efforts to turn them around and make them viable. Eventually perseverance bore fruit, the investments became profitable, and the Sandals Group became a lucrative reality. The offshoot of Beaches has also held its own in the international marketplace. Beaches was marketed as more of a family environment which now included the off- springs of the original supporters of the group who now had children and wished to have them share in their experiences. Gordon "Butch" Stewart died on January 4th, 2021, but his legacy will live on for centuries to come.

Michael Lee Chin

There are different ways that one can contribute to, and ultimately change the landscape and turn an idea into a profitable venture; and Michael Lee-Chin has done just that.

Michael Lee-Chin, born on January 3rd, 1951, is reported by Wikipedia as at March 2018, as being the 20th richest man in Canada with a net worth of Can $3.95 billion. This is no small feat and could only have been achieved by realizing the potential of one's dream and sticking with it to the end.

Lee-Chin is the Chairman and CEO of Portland Holdings Inc. which has its headquarters in Ontario Canada. A.I.C was acquired by Lee-Chin in 1987 when it had less than one million ($1M) in assets under management. The wealth management company managed over $10 billion in assets by 2002. In the recession of 2008, A.I.C was sold to Manulife. In 2017 the Order of Ontario was bestowed on him, which is the province's highest honour, thereby recognizing him as an Ontarian who has made material contributions to the province.

A Jamaican by birth, Lee-Chin's philanthropy spanned over the ocean to his native country where he is reported to have made considerable wealth investing in Natural Commercial Bank. The Jamaican Economic Growth Council appointed him Chairman in 2016. It is reported that the 65% stake he has in National Commercial Bank now makes up for the majority of his wealth.

In Canada, Lee-Chin has made sizeable contributions to several institutions, including but not limited to: Joseph Brant Hospital, Royal Ontario Museum, McMaster University, and The Rotman School of Management at the University of Toronto. Lee Chin has also served in the capacity of Chancellor at Wilfred Laurier University.

Profiles of Other Noteworthy Entrepreneurs

- **Audrey Hinchcliffe,** head of Manpower and Maintenance Services Ltd. She was also invited by former United States Secretary of State Hillary Clinton to join the US

Department of State's International Council on Women's Business Leadership for a two-year term. Hinchcliffe is principal of Caribbean Health Management Consultants Limited.

- **Phillip Gore,** Executive chairman of Gore Developments, who has received many awards for his work in shaping the construction industry and for contributing to the economic development of Jamaica. He is also well known for charity work.

- **Glen Christian,** Chairman and founder of Cari-Med and Kirk Distributors whose experience spans more than 40 years working in the pharmaceutical consumer goods industries. At that time, Cari-Med had a staff compliment of 380 as one of the leading pharmaceutical companies in the Caribbean.

- **Basil Johnson,** a self-made businessman, founder and managing director of Montego Bay-based Discount Lumber & Hardware Limited, Discount Lumber Limited, and Discount Mart Limited.

Informal Commercial Trading

We could not close this section without highlighting a segment of the business sector that contributes to the greatness of our people, namely the Informal commercial trading. This is an important aspect of the Jamaican economy, particularly in urban areas where it is a common source of income for many people. Informal traders in Jamaica are typically individuals or small groups who sell goods and services without a formal license or registration, often on the street or in markets.

Informal commercial trading in Jamaica is a diverse and dynamic sector, encompassing a wide range of goods and services, including clothing, food, electronics, and other consumer goods. It is estimated that the informal sector accounts for a significant portion of the Jamaican economy, with some estimates suggesting that as many as 70% of small businesses in Jamaica operate in the informal sector.

While informal commercial trading can provide an important source of income for many people in Jamaica, it is also associated with a number of challenges and risks. Informal traders often operate in challenging conditions, including lack of access to credit, limited legal protections and limited access to basic services such as health care and education. In addition, informal traders in Jamaica face a range of regulatory and legal challenges, including restrictions on where they can sell their goods and services, and frequent crackdowns by law enforcement. Despite these challenges, informal commercial trading continues to be an important part of the Jamaican economy, providing employment and income for thousands of people across the island.

We have mentioned in this chapter some of the giants in the business community but must also pay homage to a group of people who have been the mainstay of the ordinary Jamaicans and are the backgrounds of our island living. They are small entrepreneurs who have daily and weekly contributed to the economy and provide a valuable service. Respect must be given to the jelly Man, the Pan Chicken man at Liguanea, and all over Jamaica, the man who sells soup by the roadside, the food man who drives his van around from community to community selling his products, and the people who sell corn and crabs at Heroes Circle. The little shops in the communities, Faith's Pen in Linstead, Pork Pit in Montego Bay, Boston Jerk Centre in Portland, and so many others, Big Up!

Chapter 9
Churches in Jamaica

Jamaican's motto is Out of Many One People, and it would therefore stand to reason that in the same way our population is made up of diverse cultures, the religious denominations, by extension, would be equally diverse. In the earlier years, Christians made up the majority of the population and our forefathers placed great emphasis on going to church, being Christian, and by virtue of that we should show respect and love to all human beings. Continued migration to our shores have brought with it, different religious point of views and hence a variety of churches, each depicting its own religious persuasions. Nevertheless, Christianity remains the predominant religion in Jamaica. See the religious affiliation chart on page 82 depicting the breakdown by percentages. Although this was based on a study done in 2011, nothing much has changed in 2023.

Religious affiliation (2011)

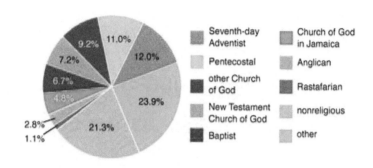

© Encyclopædia Britannica, Inc.

There are other religious denominations that form part of the population, such as worshipers of, Islam, Baha'i, Buddhism, Sikhism, and Hinduism.

The Seventh Day Adventist Church in Jamaica

The Seventh-day Adventist Church in Jamaica is a Christian denomination that is part of the worldwide Seventh-day Adventist Church. It is one of the largest Protestant denominations in Jamaica, with over 320,000 members and approximately 710 churches and congregations throughout the island.

The Adventist Church was first introduced to Jamaica in the late 19th century by American missionaries, and it has since grown rapidly. Today, the church has a significant presence in the country, with many of its members actively involved in various community outreach programs and humanitarian efforts.

In addition to its spiritual mission, the Seventh-day Adventist Church in Jamaica is also known for its emphasis on health and wellness. The denomination operates several hospitals and clinics across the country, providing healthcare services to people regardless of their religious affiliation.

The Adventist Church in Jamaica also places a strong emphasis on education, with many of its members attending Adventist-run schools and colleges. In fact, the church operates the Northern Caribbean University, which is one of the largest private universities in the Caribbean.

Overall, the Seventh-day Adventist Church in Jamaica has had a significant impact on the country, both spiritually and socially. Its members are actively involved in various aspects of Jamaican society and the denomination has become an important part of the island's cultural and religious landscape.

The Catholic Church in Jamaica

Holy Trinity Cathedral -
A Roman Catholic Church in Jamaica

The Catholic Church in Jamaica is a Christian denomination that is part of the worldwide Catholic Church. It is a relatively small denomination in Jamaica, comprising only about 3% of the country's population. However, it has a rich history in the country and has played an important role in the development of Jamaican society.

The Catholic Church was first introduced to Jamaica by Spanish colonizers in the 16th century, and it has since grown to become a significant presence on the island. Today, the Church has 3 dioceses in Jamaica: the Archdiocese of Kingston, the Diocese of Montego Bay and the Diocese of Mandeville.

One of the Catholic Church's most prominent institutions in Jamaica is the University of the West Indies, which was founded in 1948 by the Catholic Church along with other Christian denominations. The Church also operates several primary and secondary schools across the country, as well as a number of healthcare facilities, including hospitals and clinics.

The Catholic Church in Jamaica is also known for its social justice work, with many of its members involved in community outreach programs and efforts to combat poverty and inequality. The Church has been vocal in advocating for human rights and social justice in the country, particularly in areas such as immigration reform and prison reform.

Generally, the Catholic Church in Jamaica has made significant contributions to the country's religious, social, and educational landscape. Despite its relatively small size, the Church has played an important role in the development of Jamaica and continues to be a prominent religious institution in the country.

The Anglican Church in Jamaica

St. Andrew Parish Church
An Anglican church in Jamaica

The Anglican Church in Jamaica is a Christian denomination that is part of the worldwide Anglican Communion. It is one of the oldest Christian denominations in Jamaica, with a history that dates back to the 17th century.

The Anglican Church was first introduced to Jamaica by British colonizers and it has since grown to become a significant presence on the island. Today, the Church has two dioceses in Jamaica: the Diocese of Jamaica and the Cayman Islands, and the Diocese of Montego Bay. It is also a member of the Jamaica Council of Churches, which is an organization that represents various Christian denominations in the country.

The Anglican Church in Jamaica operates a number of schools, including several primary and secondary schools, as well as theological colleges and seminaries. The Church also has a significant presence in the healthcare sector, operating several hospitals and clinics throughout the country.

One of the Anglican Church's most well-known institutions in Jamaica is the historic Kingston Parish Church, which was built in the 17th century and is one of the oldest churches on the island. The Church has also been involved in various community outreach programs, including efforts to combat poverty and promote social justice.

The Anglican Church in Jamaica has played an important role in the country's religious, social, and educational landscape. Its members are active in various aspects of Jamaican society, and the Church continues to be an important religious institution in the country.

The Baptist Church in Jamaica

Mandeville Baptist

The Baptist Church in Jamaica is a Christian denomination that has a significant presence in the country. It is one of the largest Protestant denominations in Jamaica, with a history that dates back to the early 19th century.

The Baptist Church was first introduced to Jamaica by British missionaries and it has since grown rapidly. Today, the Church has over 400,000 members and is represented by various organizations and associations, including the Jamaica Baptist Union and the Jamaica Baptist Women's Federation.

The Baptist Church in Jamaica operates a number of schools, including primary and secondary schools, as well as a theological college. It is also involved in various community outreach programs and social justice initiatives, including efforts to combat poverty and promote human rights.

One of the most prominent institutions associated with the Baptist Church in Jamaica is the Jamaica Baptist Convention Centre, which is located in Kingston and serves as a hub for various Baptist-related activities and events. The Church is also known for its emphasis on evangelism and missionary work, both within Jamaica and in other parts of the world.

The Baptist Church in Jamaica has had, and continues to have, a significant impact on the country's religious and social landscape. Its members are involved in various aspects of Jamaican society and the Church continues to be a prominent religious institution in the country.

Rastafarianism in Jamaica

Rastafarianism is a religious movement that originated in Jamaica in the early 20th century. It is a syncretic religion that draws on a variety of cultural and religious influences, including elements of Christianity, African spirituality, and the teachings of Marcus Garvey, a Jamaican political activist and Black Nationalist.

Rastafarianism is best known for its distinctive cultural practices and symbols, which include the wearing of dreadlocks, the smoking of ganja (marijuana) as a sacrament, and the use of

Rastafarian colors (red, gold, and green) in clothing and decorations.

Rastafarianism has had a significant impact on Jamaican culture and society, particularly in the areas of music and art. The movement has inspired many Jamaican musicians, including Bob Marley, Peter Tosh, and Burning Spear, who have used their music to promote Rastafarian beliefs and values. Rastafarian art, which often incorporates the movement's symbols and motifs, has also become an important part of Jamaican cultural expression.

Rastafarianism has also played a role in Jamaican politics and social activism. The movement's emphasis on black liberation and empowerment has inspired many Jamaicans to take a more active role in advocating for social justice and political change.

Despite its cultural and social significance, Rastafarianism has faced some challenges in Jamaica, including discrimination and persecution from the government and mainstream society. However, the movement continues to be an important part of Jamaican culture and identity, and its influence can be seen in many aspects of Jamaican life.

Pocomania in Jamaica

Pocomania is a syncretic religious movement that originated in Jamaica in the late 19th century. It is a blend of African, European and indigenous spiritual traditions, and is similar in some ways to other Afro-Caribbean religions, such as Santeria and Voodoo

The name "Pocomania" is believed to have originated from the Spanish word "poco" meaning "little," and "mania" meaning "madness." The movement is known for its ecstatic worship, which includes the use of music, dance, and possession by spirits.

Pocomania is primarily practiced in rural areas of Jamaica, and its rituals often involve elements of nature, such as water and fire. The religion places a strong emphasis on healing and spiritual protection; and its practitioners often wear special clothing and accessories, such as head wraps and charms, to ward off evil spirits.

Pocomania has faced some challenges in Jamaica, including persecution and discrimination from mainstream society, However, the movement continues to be an important part of Jamaican cultural heritage, and has inspired a number of important cultural expressions, including music, dance, and art.

CHAPTER 10
Professionals Locally and in the Diaspora

Jamaica has a well-educated workforce and many Jamaicans have excelled in their chosen professions, making valuable contributions to their communities and society at large. Additionally, many Jamaican professionals have established successful careers and businesses both at home and abroad, contributing to the economic growth and development of their communities, the country, and the world at large. In the Diaspora, Jamaican professionals have made significant contributions to their adopted countries, becoming leaders in various fields and disciplines. They have also remained connected to their Jamaican roots and have supported various initiatives and organizations that benefit the Jamaican community.

Generally, Jamaican professionals are a vital and valuable part of the country's social, economic, and cultural landscape, and their contributions are essential to the continued growth and development of Jamaica and its global community.

Jamaica and its Diaspora are home to a diverse range of professions and professionals. Here are some examples of the range of professions and professionals in Jamaica and the Jamaican Diaspora:

Healthcare professionals: Jamaica and its Diaspora are home to a wide range of healthcare professionals, including doctors, nurses, pharmacists, and other allied health professionals.

Teachers and educators: There are many educators and teachers in Jamaica and its Diaspora, including those who work in primary and secondary schools, as well as those who work in higher education.

Artistes and musicians: Jamaica has a rich cultural heritage, and it is home to many talented artists and musicians. Jamaican artists and musicians have made significant contributions to the global arts scene.

Business professionals: Jamaica and its Diaspora are home to many business professionals, including entrepreneurs, executives and managers. Many Jamaicans have started successful businesses both in Jamaica and abroad.

Lawyers and legal professionals: Jamaica and its Diaspora are also home to many legal professionals, including lawyers, judges, and legal assistants.

Engineers and scientists: Jamaica and its Diaspora have many engineers and scientists, including those who work in the fields of civil engineering, mechanical engineering, electrical engineering, and computer science.

Financial professionals: Jamaica and its Diaspora have many financial professionals, including bankers, accountants, and financial analysts.

Journalists and media professionals: Jamaica has a vibrant media industry and it is home to many journalists, editors, and other media professionals.

Overall, Jamaica and its Diaspora are home to a wide range of professions and professionals, reflecting the country's diverse economy and rich cultural heritage. We'll highlight five outstanding professionals in the Science Technology Engineering and Mathematics [STEM] field, who are making a huge difference internationally, further highlighting the greatness of our people.

Dr. E Dale Abel

Dr. Abel, MD, PhD is president elect of the International Endocrine Society. Evan dale Abel was born in 1963 and studied at the University of West Indies before transitioning to Oxford University. Doctor Abel has had an outstanding career and is the recipient of a multitude of honors and awards. Listed below are some of his achievements:

- 1986—Rhodes scholarship from the University of Oxford.
- 1996-Harvard Medical School, 50th University Scholars in Medicine Fellowship.
- 1999—Harvard Medical School Excellence in Teaching Award.
- 2001- American Thyroid Association Van Meter Award.
- 2001—David W. Haack Memorial Award in Cardiovascular Research.
- 2003—Established Investigator of the American Heart Association.
- 2012—Meharry Medical College James Pulliam Memorial Lectureship.
- 2012-Endocrine Society Gerald D. Aurbach award Lecture
- 2013—Elected Fellow of the American Heart Association.
- 2015—university of Tennessee Health Science Center the Max Miller Lecture
- 2015—Elected to the National Academy of Medicine.
- 2018—NIH Director Astute Clinical Lecture.
- 2018—African American Museum of Iowa History Makers Award.
- 2020—Selected as President -Elect of the Association of professors of Medicine.
- 2020—Named by Cell Press as one of the most inspirational Black scientists in the United States.

Dr. Abel has published books including, *Diabetic Cardiomyopathy, Causes and Effects*, and *Diabetic Cardiomyopathy Revisited.*

Dr. Winston Dawes

Dr. Winston "Cubba" Dawes, M.B.B.S, F.R.C.S.E., CD, has had an outstanding career in the field of medicine in Jamaica, and has also made invaluable contribution to sports in an administrative capacity, and also in the field of sports medicine.

Dr. Dawes served as Senior Medical Officer of the Morant Bay Hospital in 1972, The Kingston Public Hospital between 1971-1975, and 1979-1982; and the May Pen Hospital from 1975-2008. Professional accomplishments are inclusive, but not limited to:

- Former Vice-President Jamaica Administrative Athletics Association.
- Director CHASE Fund
- Former Vice President, Jamaica Olympic Association
- Past President Medical Association of Jamaica

- Former President, Jamaica Football Association
- Member Medical Council of Jamaica
- Member Jamaica Association of Sports Medicine
- Past Chairman Insport
- Past Chairman G.C. Foster College
- Member American College of Sports Medicine

Dr. Dawes presently hosts the RJR 94FM programme "Doctors Orders" and is the Chief Executive Officer of Mahogany Health &Fitness. Some of Dr. Dawes' offspring's have ventured on a similar path and thus are continuing and improving on the legacy of their renowned father in the medical profession. Dr. Alfred Dawes has charted a similar course to his father, as he heads to the Savanna-La -Mar hospital in the senior post.

Dr. Michelle Johnson

Dr Michelle Johnson is Associate Chief of Cardiology at Memorial Sloan Kettering Cancer Centre in New York. She is also one of the few doctors at the hospital who specializes in cardiovascular disease. Dr Johnson was born in Jamaica and is a graduate of Immaculate Conception High School.

Dr. Kathie-Ann Josephs

Dr. Kathie-Ann P Joseph grew up in Brooklyn New York but was born in Jamaica. Dr. Joseph is the director of breast services at Belleview Hospital. A graduate of Columbia University College of Physicians and Surgeons in 1995 and a specialist in general surgery, she is the first black woman to be appointed to the faculty of the Department of Surgery at New York Presbyterian Hospital/ Columbia University Medical center (NYPH/Columbia). She was once named by Crain's New York Business weekly as one of its 40 rising stars.

Simone Badal McCreath, PhD

Dr. Simone Badal McCreath is a leading Jamaican scientist and lecturer at the Basic Medical Science Department, Faculty of Medicine, at The University of the West Indies. Her work involves the screening of synthetic and natural compounds for chemo preventative and anticancer properties. Dr. Badal McCreath and her team of young scientists developed the first Caribbean cell line for Black men in 2021, ACRJ-PC28. She holds the Best Research Award 2013-2014 and is an author.

Dr. Badal McCreath is quite accomplished, holding a BSc (Hons), PhD, MBA and MPhil. She is an editorial board member of American International Journal of Biology, and is a reviewer of Open Access Biochemistry, London. Her lists of accolades include, but are not limited to:

- The Elsevier award for early career women scientist in Chemical Sciences for Latin America and Caribbean Region, 2014
- The Young Scientist/Technologist awardee at the 23rd Science and Technology Conference and Expo in 2010,
- The Inaugural Luther Speare Scholar from the University of The West Indies Mona in 2010

One of Dr. Badal McCreath's focuses is isolating Jamaican plants that may have anti-cancer properties, in order to create a unique Jamaican cell line.

Chapter 11

Cultural Foods, Drinks, Delicacies

You may ask, what is the correlation between slavery, our foods, fruits, herbs, medicinal roots and the delicacies we have become accustomed to enjoying? In the days of slavery, until the present day, the inhabitants of the land have had to live on the fruits grown and also use the herbs and other medicinal roots for healing in the absence of available medical personnel and medicine. It would therefore be remiss of me not to mention these gems which were all used to sustain and heal our people. Slavery had instilled in us some survival skills and encouraged us to be self-sufficient and to live off the land. We also need to make mention of the link that needs to be made between our African ancestry and the foods we now eat. Let's now have a brief look at some of these treasures, most of which are treasures emanating from our past.

Jamaican cuisine is known for its bold and flavorful dishes, influenced by African, European and Asian culinary traditions.

The transition from slavery brought with it norms, traditions and cultural practices, religions, and foods that still resonate with us today.

Rice and Peas: This is a staple side dish in Jamaica, made with rice and red kidney beans cooked in coconut milk and seasoned with thyme, garlic, and scallions.

Fried Ripe Plantains: These are a popular Jamaican side dish made by frying ripe plantains until they are crispy and carame-lized.

Coconut Drops: This is a popular Jamaican snack made from coconut sha-vings, brown sugar, and ginger, formed into small candy-like drops.

Jamaican Patty

This is a pastry filled with meat or vegetables and seasoned with Jamaican spices, often served as a quick snack or on-the-go meal. Most Jamaicans compliment a patty with coco bread and a drink, and that suffices for lunch.

Sorrel

This is a popular Jamaican drink made from the hibiscus flower, flavored with ginger, cinnamon, and other spices.

Jamaican National Dish –Ackee and Saltfish

Ackee and salt fish is Jamaica's national dish and is worthy of the title that has been bestowed on it because it is truly a delectable meal that entices and satisfies. The fruit was imported from East Africa before 1725 and is consumed both locally and overseas. The more notable canning companies package this novelty and export it to countries all over the world, but in particular, some major markets are the United States and Canada.

White Rum

Nine night or *set up*, domino game, rum bar, dance, funeral, or anywhere Jamaicans congregate, the Jamaican white rum is a type of rum that is made in Jamaica and is known for its distinctive flavor and aroma. It is made from sugar cane, which is crushed to extract the juice, which is then fermented and distilled to produce rum. The rum has evolved from a less refined state, referred to locally as "Johncrow Batty Rum",or Kulu Kulu, which was exceptionally potent, compared to the drink we now enjoy in it's very transformed, and often times, less potent state.

Blue Mountain Coffee

Jamaican Blue Mountain coffee is an exclusive type of coffee that is grown in the cool and misty Blue Mountains of Jamaica, which is the highest mountain range in the country. It is grown at elevations of 3,000 to 5,500 feet above sea level. The coffee beans are hand-picked and processed with great care to ensure the highest quality. The beans are then roasted to produce a medium-bodied coffee with a mild and smooth taste, and a bright acidity.

Jerk Chicken

Jamaica Jerk Chicken is a popular and traditional Jamaican dish that is known for its bold and spicy flavor. The dish is made by marinating chicken in a mixture of spices and seasonings, and then grilling or smoking it over pimento wood or charcoal.

Not many residents or visitors to our shore are fortunate to get the opportunity to experience firsthand, our Portland Jerk Festival. This is the Jerk capital of Jamaica and the festival is a well sought-after event which showcases the various items on display being jerked in the traditional setting and being cooked over pimento wood fires. The festival is an event which literally lights up your taste buds and serves to create an atmosphere that is not easily forgotten.

Roasted Fish

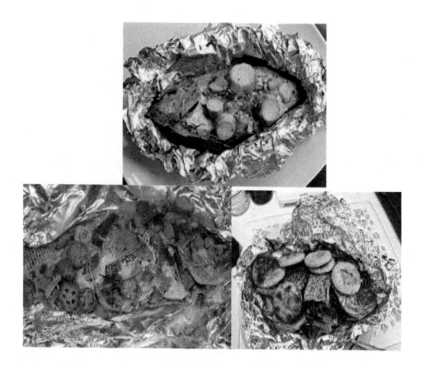

Jamaican roast fish is a popular dish in Jamaica and it is often served at any occasion, but there are special occasions, such as weddings and holidays that benefit from this delicacy. It is also a popular street food in Jamaica, with many vendors selling the dish from roadside stalls.

Jamaican roast fish is a delicious and flavorful dish that is enjoyed by locals and visitors alike. It is a great example of the diverse and scrumptious cuisine that Jamaica has to offer.

Roasted Breadfruit

The breadfruit was recorded as being brought to the island by Captain Bligh in the year 1793 from Tahiti. Since then, it has been used by Jamaicans in several different dishes and has added both substance and flavour to these meals. The fruit can be roasted, fried and boiled, depending on the sort of meal that it is being used to enhance. The boiled breadfruit is most times put in soups, but the roasted and fried breadfruit can be used to supplement a variety of dishes.

Fish and Festival or Bammy

Jamaican Festival is a type of fried dumpling –like food that is made with a combination of flour, cornmeal, sugar, and spices. The dough is shaped into small balls and rolled into discs before being deep-fried until crispy and golden brown. Festival has a slightly sweet taste and a fluffy texture and is often served as a side with savoury dishes like jerk chicken, stewed beef, fish or curried goat.

Bammy is a cassava-based product which is extremely tasty and can be steamed or fried and used to complement fish and meat dishes. Like festivals, bammy is used to complement fish dishes, which may be steamed, fried, brown stewed, or escoveitched. Both visitors and residents love this delicacy. Restaurants such as Gloria's and others in Port Royal, and restaurants near Jolly's in Portmore, attract a large following because of these dishes.

Curried Goat

Curried goat (*Curry Goat*) is a popular and beloved dish in Jamaica and is a staple of Jamaican cuisine. The dish is made by marinating goat meat in a mixture of spices and seasonings, and then slowly cooking it in a rich and fragrant curry sauce.

It is inconceivable to top the delicious descriptions, but every meal we have described on this journey may be described thusly, and, with that being said, the icing on the cake is a well-seasoned plate of curry goat and white rice. Bon Appétit.

Dukunoo or Blue Draws

Dukunoo, also known as Tie-A-Leaf, or Blue Draws, is a traditional Jamaican dessert that is made from grated green bananas, coconut, sugar, and spices, all wrapped in banana leaves and boiled until fully cooked. It may also be used to supplement a meal. Dukoono is a sweet starchy pudding that originated in

West Africa. It is extremely filling in spite of the deceiving appearance and taste of being an after meal, desert like snack. It can also be made from cornmeal, or sweet potato, and some persons are known to add raisins to supplement the taste.

Chapter 12

Jamaican Fruits & Berries

Jamaican fruits and berries and their origins

E xotic, satisfying, healthy, and tasty. These are a few of the words that may be used to describe the treasures of our collection of fruits. Growing up, children, and indeed adults, would never be hungry because the wide array of fruits that could be consumed to ward off hunger was vast. During mango season, we ate until we were gorged. The same could be said of guineps, naseberries, apples, and indeed, any other fruit. Partaking in these cultural treasures is an experience that should not be missed. Jamaica is home to a wide variety of fruits and berries that are both indigenous and introduced to the island over time. Let's look briefly at some of these treats.

Ackee

Ackee and salt fish is the national dish of Jamaica, and often times provide a staple meal for a large part of the population, who cherish this amazing dish irrespective of their background or upbringing. Ackee is native to West Africa and was introduced to Jamaica in the 1700s. It has since become a popular ingredient in many Jamaican dishes.

Guava

Guava is native to Central and South America but was introduced to Jamaica by the Spanish in the 16th century. It is a common fruit in Jamaica and is often eaten fresh or used in juices and desserts.

Star Apple

Star Apple is native to the Caribbean and was likely present in Jamaica before European colonization. It is a fruit with a unique taste and texture and is often enjoyed as a fresh fruit or used in juices and desserts.

Pineapple

Pineapple is native to South America but was introduced to Jamaica by the Spanish in the 16th century. Jamaica is known for its sweet and juicy pineapples, which are often used in drinks and desserts.

Soursop

The Soursop has been used by several cultures for both the savoury nature of its juices and also the medicinal properties of the fruit, the leaves and the bark. It is purported to possess several health benefits including the prevention of cancer, although this has not be clinically proven, or acknowledged.

Mangoes

Jamaican mangoes are extremely tasty and nutritious. They tantalize the taste buds and also offer their fair amount of Vitamin C to our diets.

Mango is seasonal and usually runs its course between April to August. It is eaten by removing the skin and devouring the delicious fruit, or used to make juice which is equally refreshing. Certain cultures have a custom of cooking the green mangoes with curry powder which also makes for an amazing dish.

Naseberries

Originally from Asia, sapodilla, or naseberry, is a sweet, succulent fruit that is popular for it's flavour and also for it's medicinal properties. It is reported that the naseberry builds immunity, supports proper respiratory functions, gives more energy, promotes healthy skin, helps with the digestive process, builds healthy bones, and is an anti-inflammatoty agent.

Guineps

Guinep is a member of the soapberry family, mostly found in the tropics, especially parts of the Caribbean and South and Central America. The guinep is borne on trees that are reported to have grown as tall as 82ft in height. The fruit is basically a stone bearing fruit, which has a juicy and somewhat stainy pulp, which usually comes in colours of salmon, orange, or a light yellow colour.

Sweet sop

It has been reported that the sweetsop is rich in sources of Vitamin B6, which helps to prevent heart disease, reduces coughing, wheezing, chest tightness, shortness of breath and bronchial inflammation. Other benefits include the prevention and relief of constipation due to its high levels of fibre, reduction of blood pressure, due to its high levels of potassium, and the lowering of the risk of type 2 diabetes. The fruit has a heart shaped appearance, and some cultures tend to subscribe to the fact that oft-times, the similarity of the shape of the fruit with an organ in the body would depict the area that would benefit most from the fruit. The sweetsop is shaped like the heart.

Jackfruit

The largest fruit to bear on trees in the world is the jackfruit, which was introduced to the island in 1782 as a result of French ships being captured and brought to Jamaica en route to Martinique.

Many vegetarians have been leaning towards the consumption of this fruit in several forms recently due to its extensive medicinal properties.

Otaheite Apple

The name Captain Bligh features prominently in Jamaican history in relation to the introduction of several fruits to the island, and the Otaheite apple is one such fruit. This fruit has been cultivated since pre-historic times, but was only introduced to the tropics in recent times. It is also considered a super food due to the amount of health benefits associated with it.

Watermelons

Watermelons are quite refreshing and a welcome thirst quencher, especially in hotter climates that are typical to our island habitat. Consisting of approximately 90% water, the fruit is nutrient packed with antioxidants, vitamin C, vitamin B6, vitamin A, amino acids, lycopene, a nominal amount of potassium and sodium, and is fat free.

Certain studies by Texas A&M University have also posited the view that the fruit may be a contributing factor in the improvement of erectile dysfunction. A fruit with a lift? No harm in enjoying the fruit, right?

Jimbilin

The Jimbilin fruit is also known as the June plum, golden apple or ambarella. It is a tropical fruit that is native to Southeast Asia and India but is also widely grown in other tropical regions around the world, including the Caribbean. The fruit is roughly oval-shaped, has a thin, greenish-yellow skin, and the flesh is yellow, juicy and slightly tangy, with a flavor that is often described as a cross between a mango and a pineapple.

Herbs and Bush Remedies

The use of herbs in traditional healing practices became a vital part of Jamaican culture and is still widely practiced today. Many Jamaicans still rely on herbal remedies to treat common illnesses and to maintain their overall health and wellbeing.

Among the list of herbs, bush remedies, that offered, and still offer medicinal value, are Aloe Vera, Cerasee, Bissy (kola nut), Guinea hen weed, mint, fever grass, and dandelion.

Aloe Vera

Bissy   **Guinea Hen Weed**

Dandelion

Fever Grass

Mint

CHAPTER 13

Resorts and Tourist Attractions

The sense of euphoria associated with the organized and scheduled series of events packaged by the resorts and all-inclusive locations, is a necessary feature to continue to promote   and reaffirm "Brand Jamaica". The multiple tourist attractions that become conversation pieces at home and abroad, also continue to capture the hearts of those who can appreciate their rare beauty. This chapter serves to tell us a little about the origins of the industries, the revolution that brought us to where they are today and their contributions to the continued evolution of our brand.

The Landscape before the resorts

Before the development of the modern resort industry, Jamaica had a range of tourist accommodations that catered to different types of travelers. In the early days of tourism in Jamaica, the island was primarily known for its natural beauty and tropical climate and many visitors came to the island seeking a tranquil and relaxing getaway. Some of the tourist accommodations that were popular during this period included:

Guesthouses and boarding houses: These were typically small, family-run establishments that offered simple accommodations and home-cooked meals to travelers. They were often located in rural areas or in small towns and were a popular choice for budget-conscious travelers.

Villas and cottages: Wealthier travelers often opted to rent villas or cottages for extended stays in Jamaica. These properties were often ideally placed in scenic locations, such as on the beach or in the mountains and offered a high level of privacy and comfort.

Hotels: Jamaica had a number of hotels that catered to tourists, including some that were considered among the most luxurious in the Caribbean. These hotels were often located in cities or near major attractions and offered a range of amenities and services to guests.

Camping and hiking: Jamaica's rugged terrain and natural beauty made it a popular destination for outdoor enthusiasts. Hiking trails and campsites were available in the Blue Mountains and other scenic areas of the island.

The tourist accommodations in Jamaica before the development of the modern resort industry were generally smaller and more low-key than the large, all-inclusive resorts that are popular today. However, they offered a range of options for travelers seeking a relaxing and enjoyable vacation in one of the Caribbean's most beautiful destinations.

What influenced the change?

There were several factors that influenced the change from guesthouses to resorts in Jamaica. One of the primary factors was the growth of the global tourism industry in the mid-20th century. This led to an increase in the number of visitors to Jamaica and created a demand for larger, more sophisticated tourist accommodations that could cater to a wide range of travelers.

In addition, Jamaica's government actively promoted the development of the tourism industry as a means of boosting the country's economy. In the 1960s and 1970s, the government introduced tax incentives and other measures to encourage the construction of large hotels and resorts in the country. This helped to attract foreign investment and to create jobs in the tourism sector.

Another factor was the changing preferences of travelers. As air travel became more affordable and accessible, tourists began to seek out more luxurious and all-inclusive accommodations that offered a wide range of amenities and activities. The development of large resorts allowed hotel operators to offer more services and amenities, such as swimming pools, restaurants, and on-site entertainment.

Finally, the development of large resorts was also driven by economies of scale. Building a large, all-inclusive resort allowed hotel operators to spread fixed costs over a large number of rooms, which made the overall cost per room more affordable. This allowed resorts to offer lower prices to guests, which made them more competitive in the global tourism market.

Phasing out the old and introducing the new

The newly established resorts in Jamaica played an important role in the country's growth and development. They are a major contributor to the country's economy, providing employment opportunities, generating revenue, and attracting foreign investment. The general benefits that are associated with the introduction of these resorts are similar in nature, and are listed below:

Employment: Resorts are one of the largest employers in Jamaica, providing jobs for thousands of people in various roles, including housekeeping, food and beverage service, management, and entertainment. The companies are known for offering competitive wages and benefits to their employees.

Tourism industry: Resorts are a significant contributor to Jamaica's tourism industry, which is a crucial sector for the country's economy. The company's resorts attract thousands of tourists to Jamaica every year, which has a positive impact on the country's foreign exchange earnings and subsequently, the bottom line. .

Environmental impact: Resorts have been recognized for their commitment to sustainability and environmental stewardship. The companies have implemented a range of environmentally friendly practices, including reducing water and energy consumption, implementing recycling programs, and promoting local agriculture.

Community impact: Resorts have a significant impact on the local communities in which they operate. The companies have implemented a range of initiatives to support the communities around their resorts, including providing funding for schools, healthcare, and social programs. They also source many of their goods and services from local businesses, which has a positive impact on the local economy.

Philanthropy: Resorts are known for their philanthropic efforts, including supporting various charities and social programs in Jamaica and other Caribbean countries. Some of the entities have also established foundations and non-profit organizations that focus on community development, education and environmental protection.

In addition to generating revenue and creating jobs, the resorts also help to promote Jamaica as a travel destination. They attract visitors from around the world, which helps to raise the country's profile and boost its image as a vibrant and welcoming destination.

Jamaica's Most Popular Hotels

Sandals

Gordon "Butch" Stewart founded Sandals, a group of all-inclusive resorts in 1981. Sandals Resorts International now has properties throughout Jamaica, Turks & Caicos, Grenada, Barbados, Antigua, the Bahamas and St. Lucia. The group boasts resorts including 16 Sandals, one Grand Pineapple Beach Resort, one Fowl Bay private island resort, four villa properties in Jamaica, and three Beaches Resorts.

Super Clubs

Six all-inclusive hotels in Jamaica make up the Super Clubs chain. These are Breezes Golf and Beach Resort, Breezes Montego Bay, Hedonism 2 in Negril, and Hedonism 3 in Runaway Bay, Grand Lido Braco, and Grand Lido Negril. The all-inclusive feature of the resorts includes but is not limited to: all you can eat, all you can drink, all entertainment, land and water sports, airport transfers, and free weddings. Water sports include windsurfing, snorkelling, kayaking, sailing, and trips on glass bottom boats.

Bahai Principe

The Bahai Principe is an all-inclusive resort in Runaway Bay which creates an environment that offers fine cuisine, lovely beaches and an exhilarating atmosphere that caters to the whole family. Equipped with a new water park for the kids, a range of water sports and a golf course for the adults, make the complete all-inclusive experience a delightful one.

The night life also holds captivating entertainment, including a karaoke piano bar; and disco dancing to Caribbean rhythms, and the latest international favourites.

Hedonism 11, Nudist Resort

The government of Jamaica built "Negril Beach Village", which eventually was renamed Hedonism 11 in 1981. It is a two-story building which was built on 22 acres of land and has 280 rooms. Super Clubs acquired an interest in 1989, until 2013 when it was sold to Marshmallow Limited. Hedonism has become popular due to its wild and provocative nudist attractions. It is an adult hotel that lends to persons who subscribe to the freedom of a liberated, unrestricted vacation. **ADULTS ONLY!**

Grand Palladium

The Grand Palladium is a group of resorts which have locations in Mexico, Brazil, Dominican Republic, Jamaica, Italy and Spain. The resorts are configured to facilitate both adults and children and offer a swim up bar, an infinity pool, hydro massage bathtubs and suites with private terraces and balconies. Among the services offered is the hosting of weddings in this romantic and lovely facility. Quite a romantic getaway for those who are so inclined.

The resorts in Jamaica have had a significant impact on the country's economy and the emergence of the people. The resort industry has also created a significant number of jobs in Jamaica, particularly in areas such as hospitality, food service and entertainment. According to the Jamaica Tourist Board, tourism directly and indirectly accounts for over 300,000 jobs in the country.

The industry is one of the largest sources of foreign exchange earnings for Jamaica. According to the World Travel and Tourism Council, the direct contribution of travel and tourism to Jamaica's GDP was 7.4% in 2019 and was expected to rise to 7.7% in 2020. In addition, resorts generate revenue for the government through taxes and other fees.

The growth of the industry has led to the development of infrastructure in Jamaica, such as airports, highways and public utilities. This has helped to improve access to remote areas of the country and has created opportunities for economic development in these regions.

Resorts have helped to promote cultural exchange between Jamaica and other countries, as visitors come to experience the island's music, food, and traditions. This has helped to raise awareness of Jamaica's cultural heritage and has contributed to the preservation of traditional arts and crafts.

Many resorts in Jamaica have established programs to support the development of local communities, through donations to schools, hospitals, and community centres. Some resorts also provide job training and other opportunities for local residents.

The general growth of the resort industry in Jamaica has had a positive impact on the country's economy and the emergence of the people. However, it is important to note that there are also some concerns about the impact of tourism on the environment, the cultural integrity of local communities, and income inequality. As such, it is important for the government and the tourism industry to work together to promote sustainable tourism practices that benefit both visitors and local residents.

Jamaica is known for its beautiful beaches, warm weather, and rich cultural heritage,

Bob Marley Museum: The Bob Marley Museum is located in Kingston and is a must-visit for music lovers. The museum is located at the former home of Bob Marley and includes exhibits on his life and music.

Green Grotto Caves: The Green Grotto Caves are a series of limestone caves located in Discovery Bay, Jamaica. Visitors can take a guided tour through the caves and see impressive stalactites and stalagmites.

Mystic Mountain: Mystic Mountain is an adventure park located in Ocho Rios, Jamaica. Visitors can take a cable car to the top of the mountain, where they can enjoy panoramic views of the surrounding area. The park also features a water slide, bobsled ride, and zip line.

Port Royal: Port Royal is a historic town located on the southern coast of Jamaica. The town was once a notorious pirate haven and is known for its rich history and architecture. Whether you're interested in natural beauty, cultural heritage, or adventure, Jamaica has something for everyone.

Devon House: Devon House is one of Jamaica's most celebrated landmarks and provides both a historic and a culinary experience for locals and visitors alike. The mansion is an architectural creation of Jamaica's first black millionaire, George Stiebel. On the compound, we find the famous Devon House I – scream, which boasts being the best ice cream on the island. Other unique treats can be found at the Artisan Village, Devon House Bakery, La Pizzeria, Lemongrass Tea Room, the Spa, Rosie's Gallery, and other delightful experiences. This gem is truly a must visit when visiting the island paradise.

Popular Tourist Attraction Sites

Dunns River Falls

The climbing of the Dunn's River Falls is an attraction for both local residents in the island and visitor who grace our shores from time to time. People climb the falls, which usually takes about 1-1 ½ hours, normally stopping along the journey to take photographs and enjoy the ambience that is associated with this adventure. Dunn's River has a plaque, placed by the Jamaican Historical Society which explains its historical significance. It reads:

Dunn's River
Near this spot was fought
the battle of Las Chorreras in 1657
When the English defeated the

Spanish expeditionary force from Cuba.

The falls has stairs which were chiseled out by nature, facilitating the climb to the top which has been recorded as being about 180 feet high and 600 feet long. The falls finally empties out in the sea at the Little Dunn's River Beach and still has the accreditation as being the most popular falls in Jamaica. The ambience of Dunn's River has been captured in movies such as James Bond's Dr. No and other movies that sought to add the romance associated with the Caribbean and white sand beaches.

Rick's Café

How many places in the world do you think you could sit comfortably and drink exotic beverages while listening to the sound of Bob Marley, watching the sunset and seeing divers make a 35-foot dive from the cliff to the waters below? Any guesses? Let me save you the mystery. Rick's Café in Negril, Jamaica, that's where!

Rick's Café was "founded" by Richard Hershman in 1974, which was at that time merely a fishing village with very little activity and not many people. The area was known for its wonderful beaches, which later were complimented with the addition of the café, coupled with a breathtaking view of the sunset which became an international attraction.

In spite of being devastated by two major hurricanes, namely Gilbert in 1988 and Ivan in 2004, Rick's Café became bigger and better, and developed into a signature attraction for visitors from all over the island, and ultimately, all over the world.

Blue Lagoon

There are myths and stories of intrigue associated with the Blue Lagoon, all of which add to the appeal and magnetic pull for visitors both locally and internationally. Stories that tell of mysterious dragons, or sea serpents, or the fact that it was a bottomless pit, only to be disproven when divers discovered that the bottom was about 180 feet down. This island paradise was also the filming location for movies such as "The Blue Lagoon", and "Club Paradise".

Negril Beach & Negril Cliffs

Negril Beach is a 7-mile stretch of white sand that is considered one of the most beautiful beaches in Jamaica. The beach is located in the town of Negril and is known for its crystal-clear water, soft white sand, and spectacular sunsets. The beach is a popular spot for swimming, sunbathing, and water sports like snorkeling, scuba diving, and parasailing. There are also plenty of beach bars and restaurants where you can enjoy a cold drink or a delicious meal while taking in the beautiful views.

The beautiful white sand beaches add great and therapeutic value to the experience. Negril is a popular tourist destination in Jamaica. The Negril Cliffs are located on the western tip of Jamaica, near the town of Negril. The cliffs are a series of limestone formations that rise up from the ocean, providing spectacular views of the Caribbean Sea. Visitors can take a guided tour of the cliffs or explore them on their own. There are also several spots where visitors can jump into the water from various heights. The Negril Cliffs are a popular spot for cliff jumping, snorkeling, and scuba diving.

YS Falls

YS Falls is a beautiful natural attraction located in Jamaica. It is situated on the south coast of the island in the parish of St. Elizabeth, near the town of Black River. The falls are named after the river which originates in the Cockpit Mountains and flows into the Caribbean Sea.

Rafting on the Rio Grande

Rafting on the Rio Grande is an extremely serene and gratifying pleasure trip highlighted by a cruise and guided tour of the river on a bamboo raft. This expedition is available seven days per week. The Rio Grande is one of Jamaica's longest rivers and the journey starts from "Rafters Rest", and normally lasts between two to three hours.

The use of "The River" was originally for transporting bananas and other produce to the port for export. The rafts are about 4 feet wide and 25 to 30 feet long and can accommodate two adults and a child. Errol Flynn, the actor, who spent a lot of his life in Jamaica, was noted for indulging in the rafting on the Rio Grande, and helped to popularize the tour of this popular river.

Blue & John Crow Mountains National Park

The Blue Mountains are named for the blue mist that often hovers over them, while the John Crow Mountains are named after the John Crow bird that is native to the area. The mountains are known for their lush rainforests, abundant wildlife, and stunning views.

The Blue Mountain and John Crow Mountain are famous and renowned in Jamaica's culture, being, among other things, the home of our Blue Mountain Coffee. History has recorded the mountain ranges being used by the Maroons to escape the tyranny of the invaders to the island and in instances, provided a stronghold for many, many battles against the British. The Blue Mountain National Park is one of Jamaica's National Parks, and is considered a national paradise with its waterfalls, countless trails, plants, and birds, and is the home of the largest butterfly.

UNESCO has designated the Blue Mountain as a World Heritage Site, which associates it with the Great Wall of China and The Pyramids of Egypt.

Doctor's Cave Beach

Put on your adventure cap and let us spend a day at Doctor's Cave Beach in Montego Bay and revel in the euphoria that accompanies that trip. There is a whole new level of fun sprinkled with little goodies like snorkeling, water sports, beach and volleyball. Visitors take advantage of the close proximity to the shops, restaurants and other stores with artifacts, whether quaint, or current, but great collection pieces, nonetheless.

Rose Hall Great House, Montego Bay

Formerly a Jamaican Georgian plantation and thought to be one of the better great houses, Rose Hall, home of the White Witch of Rose Hall, has now been converted to a house museum. It was a story of mystery and intrigue that amplified the appeal associated with this plantation, and attracted visitors, both locally, and from overseas, to visit the site to see this treasure firsthand.

The Rose Hall Great House was the home of Annie Palmer, a wealthy plantation owner known as the "White Witch of Rose Hall." Palmer was known for her cruelty towards her slaves and was rumored to practice voodoo and other dark magic. The legend says that she killed her three husbands and that her ghost still haunts the mansion to this day.

Today, visitors can take a guided tour of the Rose Hall Great House and learn about its fascinating history. The tour takes visitors through the mansion's beautifully decorated rooms, including the dining room, drawing room and bedrooms. There are also exhibits on the history of slavery in Jamaica and the life of Annie Palmer.

Conclusion

Vision 2030 Jamaica is a long-term development plan created by the Jamaican government to guide the country's economic, social and environmental progress from 2009 to 2030. Its stated vision is to make Jamaica the place of choice to live, work, do business and raise families by 2030. The vision aims to transform Jamaica into a fully developed country with a prosperous economy, healthy society, and a sustainable environment.

This work supports that vision and appeals to Jamaicans at home and abroad, to embrace our heritage, love our fellow Jamaicans from wherever they may have originated; appreciate and respect our culture, our similarities and our differences; and be a part of the solution, and not the problem. Jamaica's evolution from slavery to now has been a long and complex journey. The country's history has been marked by the brutal legacy of colonialism, slavery and exploitation, which have left lasting scars on its people and its social, economic and political systems.

In this volume, we have traced our history and have given a brief synopsis of our origins, the trials we underwent, the challenges we have overcome and the giant we have become, having now gained international recognition and carved our niche in so many areas worthy of note. The journey and the challenges that ensued, can only be likened to the process of forging, because that is indeed the transition that our journey has been in order to arrive at where we are now.

We have been forged into who we are by championing a path affected by Slavery and Colonialism, Globalization, psychosocial effects, geo-political influences, the contributions of our national heroes, the proliferation of our music, sports, and indeed the benefits and offshoots of migration. Our fight for independence was affected by political movements, economic and international pressures, and leadership.

Today, Jamaica is a vibrant, multicultural society with a diverse population and a rich history. Despite its challenges, the country has shown resilience and determination in the face of adversity. As Jamaica continues to evolve and develop, it is important to acknowledge the legacy of its past and work towards a more just and equitable future for all of our people.

Ideally, we would have loved to share with you all the nuggets, whether great or small, but time will not allow us in this episode, so maybe consideration will be given for another time. We can be proud of our legacy as Jamaicans at home, and in the Diaspora. We must continue to embrace, and nurture our legacies and continue to proclaim, "Jamaica, Jamaica, Jamaica Land we Love". Thank you for sharing with us this remarkable journey and as Louise Bennett (Miss Lou) would say, 'until next time, walk good".

About the Author

Courtney St. Bernard Hutchinson is a graduate of Calabar High School and Wolmer's Boys' School. He chose to put on hold his law career, which was slated to commence at Cave Hill Campus in Barbados, to pursue business. Since then, he spent most of his life seeking to bridge gaps between the accomplished and the underachievers.

Having done management courses to remain relevant in his current field, he became Operations Manager for an international organization, then Operations Director for another, until he eventually worked with Business Recovery Services Limited, which specialized in Temporary Management, Receiverships and Liquidations.

Courtney migrated to Canada in 2013 and decided, among other things, to pursue his passion for writing. He started out using poems and short stories and now he has penned his debut book, "**The Greatness of a People: The Jamaican Story.**" Through this book, he seeks to sensitize, educate, and encourage people who have not had the privilege of enjoying the treasures of this island paradise to see its beauty. He also aims to rekindle the flames in the heart of Jamaicans in the diaspora, who have neglected their homeland for much too long.

A proud father of three sons and an avid supporter of Jamaican track and field, Courtney now encourages you to sit back, put a leg up and savour " **The Greatness of a People: The Jamaican Story.** "

References

BBC Gossip. (n.d.). Meet Bob Marley's 12 Children – Most of Whom Followed in His Footsteps. Retrieved from https://bbcgossip.com/news/meet-bob-marleys-12-children-most-of-whom-followed-in-his-foo

Britannica. (n.d.). Marcus Garvey. Retrieved from https://www.britannica.com/biography/Marcus-Garvey

Jamaica Gleaner. (2014). 10 Outstanding Business Leaders. Retrieved from https://jamaica-gleaner.com/article/business/20140806/10-outstanding-business-leaders

Jamaica Information Service. (n.d.). Jamaican History. Retrieved from https://jis.gov.jm/information/jamaican-history

Jamaica Information Service. (n.d.). Norman Washington Manley. Retrieved from https://jis.gov.jm/information/heroes/norman-washington-manley

Jamaica Information Service. (n.d.). Andrew Michael Holness. Retrieved from https://jis.gov.jm/profiles/andrew-michael-holness

Jamaica Information Service. (n.d.). Sir Donald Sangster: A Legacy of Distinguished Service. Retrieved from https://jis.gov.jm/features/sir-donald-sangster-a-legacy-of-distinguished-service

Jamaica Information Service. (n.d.). Herbert Henry McKenley. Retrieved from https://jis.gov.jm/information/famous-jamaicans/herbert-henry-mckenley

Larsoon, P. 2023. Top10 Historical World 100 and 200m rankings. Retrieved from

http://www.alltime-athletics.com/m_100ok.htm

Wikipedia. (n.d.). Prime Ministers of Jamaica. Retrieved from https://en.wikipedia.org/wiki/Prime_Minister_of_Jamaica

Wikipedia. (n.d.). Bob Marley and the Wailers. Retrieved from https://en.wikipedia.org/wiki/Bob_Marley_and_the_Wailers

Wikipedia. (n.d.). Religion in Jamaica. Retrieved from https://en.wikipedia.org/wiki/Religion_in_Jamaica

Wikipedia. (n.d.). Don Quarrie. Retrieved from https://en.wikipedia.org/wiki/Don_Quarrie